Haunted History Tours
presents

New Orleans

Ghosts, Voodoo & Vampires

Kalila Katherina Smith

Fifth edition

ISBN 1-883100-04-6

Published by De Simonin Publications
P.O. Box 57223
New Orleans, LA 70157
Printed in the USA
$14.95

Photography by Sidney Smith
Edited by Renee Dodge

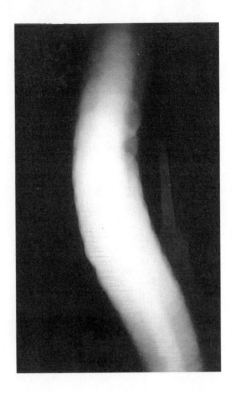

Dedicated to those who believe, and to those who do not...
YET!

TABLE OF CONTENTS

"Ghostbuster" Dan Aykroyd with Sidney Smith

Tour guide Eugenia Rainey

Sidney Smith, Owner

THESE ARE THE TOURS
YOU'VE HEARD ABOUT!

Haunted History Tours are regarded by many as being a "must do" for any visitor to New Orleans. In fact, *Spirit Magazine*, the in-flight publication of Southwest Airlines listed our tours as being one of *the* things to do while in our city. The Travel Channel has called us the number one tour company in New Orleans.

Natives, too, have come to regard these tours as one of our special highlights. Local publications such as the *Times-Picayune, City Business, Gambit, This Week In New Orleans, WHERE*, and *New Orleans Magazine* have also taken notice of these popular tour adventures.

In addition, CBS, NBC, ABC, CNN, ESPN, MTV, and the FOX Network have all featured Haunted History Tours within the last several years. National magazines such as *Southern Living, Maxim*, and *Orient Express* have each focused on French Quarter and Garden District expeditions as being highly recommended for anyone spending time in the Crescent City.

If this sounds like we're tooting our own horn a bit, we are! I am very proud of what we have created here. In fact, our success has even spawned several imitators in the ghost and vampire tour market. While imitation is the fondest form of flattery, I can honestly now say, when it comes to this subject...

WE WROTE THE BOOK!

This book was created in response to simple demand. Many people who take our tours walk away in awe, but also with fervor for additional knowledge. This body of work comprises the most definitive information to date on hauntings and vampiric activity in our city.

As you peruse these pages, you, too, will come to understand why New Orleans is regarded by many to be the most haunted city in North America.

Sidney Smith
Owner, Haunted History Tours, Inc.

We welcome your comments, suggestions and personal experiences from taking our tours.

Please write to us at: Haunted History Tours

97 Fontainebleau Drive
New Orleans, LA 70125

or E-Mail us at: webmistress@hauntedhistorytours.com
or contact us by phone: call (504)861-2727 or Toll Free (888) 6-GHOSTS

Happy Hauntings!

Sidney Smith and Midian von Thorne on a radio interview

Tour guide Mike Dardant displaying the book to tour participants

Ecto on Royal Street

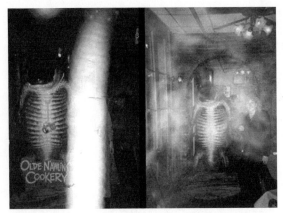

Ecto appearing in photo at Olde Nawlins Cookery

Introduction

*N*ew Orleans has been called the most haunted city in the United States. The stories in this book are from our French Quarter Ghost Tour, our Ghosts of the Garden District Tour, our Voodoo Tour and our Vampire Tour. Please keep in mind that all of these stories are based on fact, not fiction. It has been said by many that the actual history of New Orleans is far stranger than anything fiction writers can create. Paranormal investigations, police reports, personal accounts and our city's archives have documented these stories.

Haunted History Tours is the only tour company in the City of New Orleans that actually researches and investigates the stories we share. Many have tried to imitate our success. We, however, have actually witnessed and documented these hauntings. We interview people who have experienced these encounters, stay overnight in haunted buildings and spend countless hours delving into archives to give accurate information. We are constantly updating information and adding new stories as we continue our research. Our use of special equipment to measure the energy and then photograph it to complete the documentation is second to none.

The vampire tales are also backed by years of research and personal experience. Many of these stories are part of New Orleans folklore, passed down through generations by word of mouth. In many instances, names have been changed or addresses omitted to protect the privacy of surviving family members of victims, witnesses or perpetrators of these ghastly crimes.

Occasionally, particularly in hotels, the staff or management will change and new personnel are reluctant to corroborate information given by previous employees. Needless to say, some hotels and other businesses fear that confirming ghosts or vampires may harm the reputation of the property. In these cases, we are limited as to what information we may include. So, come, let the journey begin...

NEW ORLEANS
GHOSTS

Building covered in ectoplasm

Hauntings 101

*A*ccording to legend, the Indians once used this vast swamp that became New Orleans as a sacred burial place. The French believed that the geographic position of this location on the Mississippi River would prove extremely profitable for trading and, in 1718, New Orleans was founded. Thus began a history that inspired Haunted History Tours, as well as this book. Needless to say, New Orleans did not appeal to the taste of wealthy Parisians. At the time, the prisons in Paris were extremely overpopulated, so the King of France decided to relieve this problem by sending prisoners here to build the colony.

Murderers, thieves, rapists and common criminals were among the first to populate the area. Living conditions were deplorable. Harsh elements, quicksand, alligators, venomous snakes, mosquitoes and disease were rampant. The murder rate was high. Add a couple of major fires that devoured the city and many of its inhabitants, numerous hurricanes, wars, and more than twenty-seven yellow fever epidemics over the next two centuries and you have excellent conditions for ghostly activity. Violent death and strong emotions contribute greatly to this phenomenon. Most of us, once deceased, pass on peacefully to the other side. However, for those taken violently, abruptly, prematurely, without warning or embodied with strong emotions, the transition is not an easy one. Why do some remain earthbound and continue to communicate with the living?

One theory is that the murdered must remain until justice has been served or until their story has been told, so we may learn from their experience. It is theorized that those who die unexpectedly or prematurely often do not realize that they have died. Other theories state that they remain to complete unfinished business. These are actual ghosts, disembodied spirits that are earthbound. This is known as an active haunting.

For others, circumstances during the time of death cause the participants to recreate the scene of death again and again. Many of these types of hauntings are seen like a hologram, somewhat transparent. Many times it is not the spirit that remains, but rather a residual energetic impression of what occurred. This is usually created from an action or emotion that was either very strong or very repetitive. This is called a residual haunting.

Some ghosts are only audible. Others are actually seen, usually very briefly and often only in one's peripheral vision. The viewer may witness just a flash of something, many times just in the outside realm. Aromas are sometimes prevalent, as are changes in temperature, and even the actual experiencing of emotions. Most hauntings are very subtle. Usually these signs go unnoticed until very late at night or early in the morning. This is when it is the quietest and the fewest distractions are present. It is not that this activity occurs more frequently during these hours, it is simply more noticeable.

Some people are more sensitive to paranormal activity than others. Everyone, however, does have the ability. Those who are sensitive may be naturally strong in this area or perhaps have tuned into that part of them and perfected it over time. Just as any other talent of the right side of the brain, it can be a learned skill. Not all psychics tune in the same way, either. Some are more apt to have audible experiences while others may tend to have visual ones. Yet others can be empathetic, actually able to experience the emotion that is present.

Besides the use of psychic abilities, paranormal investigation can include the use of meters to measure the electro-magnetism of haunted locations. Audio and photographic equipment are sometimes used as well. Certain films will pick up impressions that cannot be seen by the naked eye. Quite often, the entity is seen as a fog or a mist on the film.

Sometimes, the actual face or figure of the entity can be seen. This is what is referred to as an apparition. On many occasions, our tour participants have captured something in one of their photographs. If this does happen, we are always happy to accept a copy for our collection. We will also analyze and research the photo and try to let you know who or what it may be. More times than not, however, catching a ghost on film requires special equipment and film, and a lot of time and patience.

Unraveling Mysteries

*I*nvestigating paranormal activity can often open doors to experiences that one might not have otherwise. On an average tour of haunted locations, it is rare for individuals to take entities home with them, although it has happened. But when you *intentionally* seek out activity, you sometimes get more than you bargained for. Over the years, I have from time to time picked up entities on properties. For the most part, these beings mean no harm and are probably just as curious about me as I am about them. Many entities, particularly those found in the French Quarter, are playful beings that seem to enjoy playing innocent pranks or simply want to be noticed.

Several years ago when I had an acupressure practice, I was setting up my treatment room in anticipation of my next client when I suddenly became aware of the strong aroma of perfume in the room. Having been on an investigation the night before, I laughed to myself and thought, "I must have picked up the ghost of one of the Storyville ladies." I sprayed air freshener and opened a door. I also politely asked the entity to leave my office and return to its origin. Several minutes later, my client arrived. During the session, he unexpectedly asked me if I was wearing perfume. He described the same fragrance I had earlier experienced. I was not sure how he would react if I told him I believed it was a ghost from the French Quarter, so I said that perhaps his treatment had accessed a repressed memory from someone in his childhood who wore that perfume. Luckily, he accepted that explanation.

Entities often have their own unique way of making their presence known to us. On another occasion one appeared in my treatment area just before a client arrived. I suspect that these particular spirits were seeking help for themselves, appearing right before a session. This spirit did not smell of perfume, but instead had a foul and obnoxious odor. Fortunately, although the entity seemed negative, it was obedient and left as requested. I have observed that spirits associated with negativity tend to reflect a lower rate of vibration. The air in the room will begin to feel heavier. With more positive beings, the sensation will be so light it feels as if one is at a higher altitude. Please understand that when I refer to these beings as "positive" or "negative," I do not necessarily mean that they are "good" or "bad." The negative vibrations could very well be from negative emotions. One can be sad, grief-stricken, depressed, guilt-ridden, angry, lonely, etc., without necessarily being malevolent. There certainly are spirits who are malevolent, but they are the minority. A negative vibration can certainly come from a spirit who is excessively needy or perhaps one who had been a substance abuser during his or her lifetime.

While most of these wandering spirits disappear readily enough if you direct them to do so, sometimes firmness is required. When the entities are spirits of children, they must be disciplined as one would a living child. The type of activity being created can often distinguish the type of spirit. Children do childish things, often to gain attention. Once given the attention they are craving, they are easily coaxed back to their "home." Most entities are attached to a specific location, article or person.

I had noticed on several occasions the ghost of a man in my home. However, during the period of time I was collecting information for this book, I encountered a very different type of entity. I was never able to distinguish who this spirit was or its origin. What made this encounter different from others I had experienced was that this entity possessed the ability not only to change its characteristics, but also to mimic characteristics of people and animals in my household. It came into my life when the first printing of this book was near completion.

During the last few weeks of writing, when I was working as long as twenty hours a day, I began to notice that everything that could possibly go wrong, did. We would spend hours editing and correcting errors in the manuscript, only to print the finished work without any of those corrections being saved. Yes, when one is working twenty hours a day it is conceivable mistakes will be made and errors overlooked, but we re-edited and corrected the *same* things over and over. Additionally, the first 2,500 copies that were printed contained errors that did not appear in the original manuscript. I spent hours scanning photographs that had virtually disappeared from the disks. It seemed that something was attempting to make it difficult for me to complete the first printing before Halloween of 1998. Fortunately, I was more determined than the entity.

It was during those final weeks that I began to notice the entity's ability to mimic. I would take much needed afternoon naps in order to work late into the night, which is more suitable to me. An afternoon nap for me is usually just relaxing with an eye pillow for about half an hour. One afternoon, as I lay in bed with my eyes covered, I felt what I believed to be my cat pouncing on the bed above my head. I even felt her circle around trying to position herself. I reached up above my head to pet her and felt nothing but a pillow. I took the eye pillow off and noticed that the cat was sitting in the hall. There was no way in those few seconds she could have gone from my pillow, through the doorway and into the hall without my seeing or feeling it.

The second incident took place a couple of days later. Again, I was lying in bed with my eyes covered. I heard what I believed to be the front door opening and closing and then what I believed to be my husband's footsteps throughout the house. I heard the steps come up the stairs and across the wood floor and stop at the edge of my bed. I specifically heard my husband's voice saying "hi." I responded by saying "hi," as I removed the eye pillow. To my astonishment, there was no one there. I rose from the bed and looked out the front window to see that my husband's car was not in the driveway. I examined the front door and found it to be bolted from the inside. I was definitely *not* asleep during these incidents. I was on call during both of these episodes and even though I was relaxing, I was still answering the phone every few minutes.

In another incident, I was awakened from a deep sleep by the entity. I had been so exhausted that I went to bed rather early that night. My seventeen-year-old stepson had gone out with friends. At about 3:00 a.m., the doorbell rang several times. I thought perhaps he had forgotten his key and was locked out. I was too tired to move, so I nudged my husband and told him that his son was locked out and to please go let him in. He very groggily got up and made his way to the front door, preparing a dissertation for the son who had so carelessly locked himself out. He discovered that not only was his son not outside, he was in his bed sound asleep. Needless to say, my husband was furious with me and accused me of hallucinating. I remain certain that I heard that doorbell ring.

On several other occasions, when I was on the third floor writing, I thought I heard that doorbell ring. This was strange because the doorbell could not be heard from the third floor. Time and time again, I would stop my writing and go down two flights of stairs only to find no one there. About a week later, we had some guests over for a party. One of my friends suddenly said that she kept hearing a doorbell but it sounded as if it was off in the distance. I made sure she repeated this to my husband to prove that my doorbell was more than just a ringing in my ears due to lack of sleep.

My husband finally became convinced that these phenomena could be attributed to paranormal activity when he experienced something himself. One morning, as I was in my daughter's room preparing her for school, I saw out of the corner of my eye what appeared to be our sheltie running past the doorway down the hall. I looked into the hall and called her but found nothing there. I soon realized that the dog was outside already and could not have passed the doorway. Later that afternoon, my husband was at our front door greeting a visitor. Suddenly he looked down and walked around in a circle, as if something was moving around him. I asked him what he was doing and he replied that he thought our dog had been running around him. I saw nothing. I still do not know who or what this spirit was. These strange events ended for *me* when this book was completed. The activity, however, seemed to follow the book itself. The woman who did my typesetting experienced similar incidents. Before working with me, she was a skeptic, but she later confided that she believed the book to be haunted. On the evening she completed the work, she insisted that she felt a "presence" in her car. She also reported seeing things out of the corner of her eye in the rearview mirror.

Of the many techniques used in our investigations, one of the most popular involves the use of psychic mediums. Mariah, a top psychic we frequently consult to assist in our investigations, has been seeing ghosts since childhood. She once told me, "If you hunt ghosts long enough, they start coming for you. We have found that a ghost is an incomplete personality. The reason there are more old ghosts than new ones is because for hundreds of years, people were instilled with the idea, 'you die, you are judged.' Many of the old ghosts fear judgment more than anything, therefore remaining in an area called the veil of illusion. Known as the white tunnel effect, they have the illusion of everything ever desired with no judgment. It is for that reason they have no desire to leave. Every earthbound ghost has a one-note cause that they want to relate to others. It is the emotional aura from the living that allows these ghosts to appear."

Mariah sensed that the ghost of the man I have seen in my house was from the 1930's. He is in his early forties, wearing a brown suit, with cuffed pants. His hair is slicked back. Mariah believed that he had wanted to be successful but probably died during the Depression. She went on to say that he loves the house, thinking it is still his. He is content with us and happy to be here.

There was also a female entity from the turn of the century detected in my house. She is in her late twenties, dressed in white lace, complete with bustle and crinoline. She is Caucasian and has brown hair, prominent eyes and fair skin. The woman married well and was well taken care of. She is intrigued with modern times, but is appalled by the way women dress today. The female ghost may be an older presence, but the male is the stronger one.

Mariah informed me that I had a portal, or doorway, in the corner of my office on the third floor. This made perfect sense because this "entrance" was situated right above my daughter's room. She had complained of sounds inside the walls. Thinking perhaps there were rats in the house, I brought in exterminators and set out bait. Still, the sounds continued at night.·

Mariah also detected a second female ghost in my office. She is a blonde woman wearing modern clothes, probably not attached to the property. Because there is a portal in this location, and because I do tend to attract spirits in my work, it is likely that she merely wandered in and decided she was comfortable here.

Mariah described what she looks for when she communicates with entities. "The doorway always opens to the left. Should one appear on the right, beware, for it is a spirit who has not yet been judged, one who haunts. An abomination is a spirit who has haunted for so long that they refuse to be judged." She went on to explain that these entities could be the most annoying to the living. They are the ones who continue to re-enact their sad issues over and over again, refusing to let go or move on. She said that one factor affecting locations where ghosts can come through is called a "ley line." Ley lines are paths of energy that surround the entire earth. These lines can be traced by linking historic landmarks such as churches, monuments and other ancient religious sites, many of which fall at the intersection of ley lines. These intersections are supposed to contain strong magnetic fields, explaining how portals are produced. It is believed that ancient people realized the power of these intersections and built their important sites there for that reason. It has also been said that these lines are the paths spirits take to travel. Mirrors situated at strategic points of the lines can strengthen the paths.

Audio equipment is also utilized in investigations. Often, the actual voices of ghosts can be picked up either digitally or on magnetic tape. During a Gothic convention in New Orleans, I had the pleasure of meeting author,

Katherine Ramsland, who just happened to be writing a book about ghost hunting. She was the first to introduce me to electronic voice phenomena, or "EVP."

On her next visit, Katherine spent a weekend with me and assisted in several investigations. She was in search of a particular ghost, one she believed to be attached to a certain piece of jewelry that she possessed. During her stay, we experimented with EVP. We set up a digital recorder in the guestroom where she was staying. During the night, the voice-activated recorder began to record what sounded like an angry male voice. We transcribed the recording as well as we could, but the entity screamed quite a bit, making it difficult to understand. It sounded as though he were saying "get out." Needless to say, this was a bit unnerving to both of us. We were unsure if this entity was someone attached to her. We were sure that none of the entities attached to the house were malevolent.

After Katherine's visit, I decided to set up the recorder in the same room one more time. Leaving the room unoccupied, I set the recorder to start at 9:30 p.m. At 1:43 a.m., the voice activation began. Once again, I heard what sounded like an angry male voice, screaming what sounded like "get out." This time, however, I noticed something else. There were other voices as well. I heard a muffled female voice. It was softer and gentler than the first one. It sounded as though they were conversing. He seemed upset and she seemed to be attempting to comfort him. In the background, I heard what sounded like whispers.

The next evening, I decided to place the recorder in a different room. This time, I set it directly in the portal on the third floor. I turned off all electronic devices and quietly placed the recorder on the corner of my desk. Although the room was completely quiet, the voice activation immediately began to record something. The following day, I checked the recording and found that the same voice and words had been recorded. This time, however, they were clearer. I turned up the volume as high as possible and slowed the voice down. I was astonished by what I was able to transcribe.

It seemed as if this entity, whoever he was, had just realized that he was dead. It is believed that spirits often remain earthbound due to either ignorance or denial of their death. With the recording slowed down, I heard that this entity was not just saying "get out," but rather, "help me get out." He kept repeating "help me, help me." He seemed to be crying at times, repeating "no, no." The female voice seemed to be trying to console him. The others mumbled softly in the background. He would scream "NOOOO!" in response to her and once even called her a liar. The entire recording lasted an hour. At one point he is crying, "Oh my God, I'm dead." He repeated this many times, screaming, getting angry, and cursing.

This clearly was not a malevolent spirit with ill intent, but a sad soul who tried in vain to get our attention for help. Once accepting his death, he would have to make a choice. He could move forward and possibly reincarnate in yet another life. Or, he could choose to remain earthbound with the others and perhaps work out his unfinished business. I decided it was best for all to let him be and allow him to work this out on his own.

Tour participant gets a surprise on her photo

Mule covered in ecto

Ghostly Attachments

Ghosts are usually associated with the properties in which they lived. They can be attached, however, not only to homes or sites but to objects or even certain people. Many times, earthbound spirits will follow a particular person or object to whom they are attached to different locations.

In the mid 1960's, a young seaman named Tony moved to the French Quarter. He soon became a fixture in French Quarter nightlife, particularly in the bars along the riverfront. Everyone in the French Quarter knew Tony and liked him. He had become a "Quarter character." But Tony had severe, uncontrollable bouts of depression. Sometimes weeks would go by without anyone seeing him. Then, once again, the sun would shine for Tony and he would be out and about in the French Quarter, laughing and socializing.

At some point, Tony stopped showing up in his regular spots. Most people figured it was just one of his spells of depression and soon he would be back on the streets. But this time several weeks went by without Tony's presence. When he failed to pay his rent at the beginning of the month, his landlord decided to enter the Decatur Street apartment to see if he had moved out. Upon opening the door of the tiny efficiency, his worst fears were realized. The stench of death was unmistakable. Tony had slit his wrists, and his decomposing body was found in the bathtub floating in blood.

For the next several years, it seemed as though the ghost of Tony remained in the tiny apartment. Resident after resident confirmed his presence. One of the most common occurrences described was that of blood sometimes appearing and then disappearing in the bathtub. The apartment had a Murphy bed, one that would fold up into the wall. Often in the evenings, the bed would open and close by itself.

Eventually the property was sold and renovated. The landlord, who had been a friend of Tony's, moved to another building and eventually opened a costume and mask shop in the French Quarter. Rather than stay in the apartment where he died, Tony's spirit moved with his former landlord and for many years resided in the costume shop. The owner of the shop often found that the masks on the wall had been mysteriously rearranged during the night.

When we first started doing tours, this was one of the first stories that we documented. When guides would stand in front of the building and talk about Tony, lights would blink inside as if he was acknowledging his story to the tour. Neighbors in nearby apartments confirmed that lights would go on and off during the night while the shop was unoccupied. The man who owned the shop passed away while this book was being written. Perhaps Tony finally crossed over with his beloved friend.

Ghostly attachments to people are one of the most common things we hear from individuals who take our tours. Sometimes we even get calls from local people who experience hauntings and want our advice.

We received one such call from a woman who had recently celebrated her daughter's birthday. She was terrified because in each photograph there was a white fog attached to her child. The party had been held in a home of a relative and she feared that the house had an entity that was attacking her child. I met with the woman and her brother to discuss the photographs. I saw that each photograph indeed had a presence attached to the woman's daughter. It did not seem to matter what was taking place or in which room, the attachment was clearly to the child. In our research we often have to rely on our psychic abilities to guide us to the answers.

As soon as I saw the photos, I felt that the ghost was not a threat to the child but a child itself. It was as if the entity was simply trying to be a part of the festivities. I asked the woman if there had been any children in the home who had died. She said that there were not. I asked if she had any children who had died and she answered no. After several questions, without getting the answers I sought, I once again asked her if she had any other children that had died possibly in a miscarriage. Suddenly, I had my answer. Her eyes filled with tears and she began to shake and cry. She stated that she had suffered a miscarriage once. Her little daughter would have had a twin! She lost the twin and carried her daughter to term. The little ghost in the photographs was there to celebrate her birthday with her sister. I reassured her that the ghost of her lost child was not there to harm her daughter but probably to be a part of the celebration. I recommended that she have another party, this time for the entity, acknowledging her as well. She was comforted and extremely grateful for what she had learned.

Other typical scenarios of attachments to property other than a location are entities that become attached to an article. We often hear from people telling us stories of buying haunted antiques from estate sales or receiving a piece of furniture that belonged to a loved one only to have the loved one still attached to it. A classic example of this is Grandma's rocker that continues to rock with no one in it.

Ghostly mist in alley

Ecto over cars

A Heaven of Their Own

Sometimes ghosts become attached to a particular location even though their death did not take place there. Perhaps it was their home, a favorite place or just a convenient stopping point.

Hello Dolly was a small doll shop located at 815 Royal Street. Inside were some of the most beautiful, unique dolls ever created. The owner, Michele Dumas, contacted us after several paranormal incidents occurred. The first disturbances she noticed were disembodied footsteps walking about the shop. A neighbor residing in the other half of the building confirmed this. Hearing the mysterious footsteps in the middle of the night, he thought the shop was being burglarized. With a gun in his hand, he approached the entrance, only to find the shop securely locked and no one inside.

Throughout the years, certain customers mentioned to Ms. Dumas that they sensed a presence in the doll shop. In one of the most bizarre occurrences, passersby have seen the figure of a man running past them and disappearing into the door of the shop. There seems to be a real sense of urgency attached to this being. The building was built in the early 1920's, and there is nothing in its history to indicate that this spirit is a previous owner. We really have no way of finding out who this man is, unless, of course, he chooses to tell us.

Le Petit Theatre was originally built in 1789 by Don Josef de Orue y Garbea, the head accountant of the Spanish Royal Finance Office and Army, to be used as his home. Fifty percent of the structure was destroyed by fire in 1794. Many of the lives lost inside this building were those of slaves. The current structure was rebuilt in the 1960's to replicate the original building. During investigations of the theatre over the years, several psychics have not only confirmed that a fire took place, but some have even reported smelling burning flesh upon entering the main theatre.

It was because of the ghosts in the theatre that I chose this location for my wedding. In the dressing room on the second floor, I could feel the presence of numerous entities, and the electro-magnetic equipment readings were extremely high. I ventured up a staircase that led to the attic. There I was met by the very strong presence of an angry male entity. The door leading to the attic was locked, so I had to wait to investigate further.

We did eventually go into the attic. Although readings remained high throughout, none of the entities there appeared on film. Mariah, a psychic who has assisted us on numerous investigations, was familiar with this building. She had been inside several times before and was quite familiar with the numerous spirits throughout. The spirits here appear not to be ghosts of those who died in the fire, but rather those of former actors who now call the theatre home. Even though they did not die here, they have congregated here in the afterlife. Mariah explained that this is where they have chosen to remain and that spending eternity in this theatre is their version of heaven.

They continue to join the living actors on stage; many of the other ghostly residents of Le Petit are former patrons who continue to sit in the theatre and enjoy the plays. Quite a few of these same ghosts congregate at One-Eyed Jacks, a club located in a building that backs up to Le Petit. The stage at One-Eyed Jacks is directly behind the wall of one of the two stages at Le Petit, giving these entities their choice of three stages to enjoy.

Ghosts often attach themselves to a particular location out of pure fear, often the fear of judgment. This seems to be the case with the Gold Club, which has been a gentlemen's club for a number of years. In the early days of New Orleans, however, it was the Borges Hotel and Saloon. Around the turn of the century, a Madame operated there who, among other things, would perform burlesque shows. She would appear on a large crescent moon that would lower her to the stage. One evening as she was making her entrance, an angry lover shot her and she fell to her death on the very spot where the stage remains to this day.

She is a very active ghost. Legends have arisen through the years of many a young man meeting and following a beautiful young woman up to her fourth floor boudoir.

Upon entering the room, they see period furniture from the turn of the century. Invited to lie down on a canopy bed covered in lace and silk, they quickly become disoriented and eventually pass out. When they awaken, they find that the woman and the room have both disappeared and they are alone in a hot, dusty attic!

I brought in Mariah to assist in an investigation of the Gold Club. Manager Chuck Rolling led us to the second floor dressing room, where some of the girls who dance there had reported sensing something. Meter readings were very high, yet sporadic. Mariah detected about three female ghosts in the area. These were girls who had previously worked at the old Borges Saloon and apparently had died at a young age. Mariah believes that these entities feel safe at this location and this is why they remain there.

Chuck then escorted us up to the attic. It was a very hot day, the heat index in the attic being at least 105 degrees, so we knew we would not be able to stay very long. Meter readings were incredibly high and we instantly felt the Madame's presence. Mariah began to describe a short, full-figured woman who was considered very attractive in her time. Sweat poured from her as she continued to describe the entity. Suddenly, I began to feel an icy presence around me. My skirt blew gently as though in a breeze. I knew for sure there was no air circulating in this stifling attic. As her presence engulfed me, I began to channel her. She was delighted that we were there for her. All she really wanted was to be acknowledged and recognized. She knew we would tell her story. She danced around us, in a whimsical, childlike fashion. Then, just as we pulled out our cameras, she quickly disappeared. For whatever reason, she was not willing to allow us to photograph her. Still, I walked away having had the most profound paranormal experience of my life. No photograph could possibly depict the emotions that were channeled through us that day.

Later that afternoon, we investigated the building that is home to Hooters restaurant. The manager, Terry, had called us after a spirit appeared in a photograph of their kitchen staff. Terry informed us that on several evenings, he had seen the figure of a woman looking down from a third floor window as he locked up the building. The upper floors were all but gutted, and it looked as if they had not been occupied for decades. Windows were broken out and pigeons had begun to make their home on the third floor. This is where we found our ghostly woman. The meter readings went up just as Mariah tuned into her.

The building, constructed in the 1800's, had been a fish house and produce market and, later, a less than reputable boarding house. This woman had been a servant there. She had no education and by our standards would be considered mentally disabled. Her master had raped her, and she bore a son who had apparently died at birth. She remains in the building, continuing to search for her child. Having lived in a world where she was considered less than human, she feared moving on, afraid that she would be judged for a crime committed against her. Fearing hell and damnation, this poor soul remains frozen in time, hoping to be reunited with a child she never knew.

We found some rather contemporary ghosts in the nightclub of Chris Owens at 500 Bourbon Street. Sol and Chris Owens bought the building many years ago. Ms. Owens has run a successful nightclub act for years and has become a New Orleans icon. An employee told us that the late Mr. Owens was believed to still "reside" in the building. She informed us that after Ms. Owens performs at night, when the club is closed, employees smell cigar smoke and sometimes feel a pat on the back for a job well done. This is exactly what Mr. Owens would do each evening after his wife's shows.

Famous trumpet player Al Hirt appeared so often in Ms. Owens' club that his name was also written across the back of the stage. Shortly after his death, employees reported seeing him sitting in the back of the stage just as he did between performances during his life. It was too soon to know if he would choose to remain in this location, or if his appearance was merely a farewell to those who knew and loved him. For many years, the back of the building has been apartments. One of those apartments had a distinctly negative presence, one that even discouraged other renters from staying there. A rather antisocial gentleman had occupied that particular apartment, had a heart attack and died on the floor while reaching for the front door.

When we entered the apartment, I inadvertently stood in the very place the man died. I did not need equipment to substantiate this haunting! Within seconds, I began to feel sick and dizzy. I suddenly felt as if my chest was caving in, and I was short of breath. I had to leave the room, and it took me about 45 minutes after departing to feel normal again. The emotions were so intense that any sensitive individual exposed to the area could experience the sensations that this man felt in his last terrifying minutes.

Sometimes, individuals spend so much of their lives in a particular location that they just do not know how to leave. This may well be true of the ghost who occupies Ralph & Kacoo's Restaurant. The management contacted us and reported that often when the restaurant was closed, the sound of toilets flushing could be heard. One employee told us that he frequently felt a presence in the back dining room. On one occasion, he saw someone quickly dart across the doorway, only to disappear.

We investigated the building and found that the energy seemed to be centered in that dining room. There we found high meter readings and temperature changes, as well as a musty odor that had not been present elsewhere. In the areas where the meter readings were the strongest, the odor was also stronger. The concentration of energy was also prevalent in an apartment directly above the dining room.

This history of the building essentially revealed the story. The building had been a parking lot in the 1970's. A clothing manufacturer had been located there from 1927 through 1967, and prior to that it had been an iron works and a rice mill. In 1844, however, it was the home of Joseph Mazza and his family. Mr. Mazza died in 1881, leaving the home to his daughter, Judith, who left the home to her children who ultimately sold it. We believe that Mr. Mazza still considers this building to be his beloved home.

This seemed to be the case, as well, at Urban Earth, an art and plant gallery located at 1528 Jackson Avenue in the Garden District. This building had for many years been used by the State as a residential mental facility. Sometimes as many as thirty residents at a time occupied this house. Activity was found in only two areas. The first was a downstairs room which had once been the recreation room for the hospital. The other was the apartment upstairs where the residents' rooms had been located.

The building was later used as an abortion clinic and family planning center. David Rengers, one of the owners of the gallery, shared some of his experiences with us. He said that on several occasions he had heard the mumbling of a woman's disembodied voice that seemed to be drifting through the old recreation room. He has also seen someone walking past an open doorway at times he knew he was there alone. One afternoon while standing outside the building, he witnessed a shadow passing in front of one of the upstairs windows. Again, no one else was there at the time.

His partner, Phil, who lived in the upstairs apartment, shared similar experiences. He said that when he first acquired the building, all the windows had been painted shut. They were the old crank type windows and most of them were broken or rusted shut and completely inoperable. One day, as he and Phil stood on the sidewalk across the street, they saw that one of those unusable upstairs windows had been opened! When they got upstairs they observed that not only had the window opened in spite of having no crank, it had been latched and subsequently unlatched by someone or something other than them. There were extremely high meter readings in all of the upstairs rooms. I felt that several presences were in the house, none of which were malevolent.

Previous tenants who owned a dressmaking shop reported similar experiences. One of them told us about an incident where a figure seated in a wheelchair appeared and remained in the room for about twenty minutes. She added that they were also frequented by a misty, white female who would appear on Christmas Day. Originating in the hallway, she would make her way to the stairs where she would sit and cry. Other activity in the building included the old elevator moving by itself, doors slamming, the sound of furniture being dragged across the floors and occasional screams.

Former site of Hello Dolly

The Bells of 1788 (617 Chartres Street)

$\mathcal{M}$any people believe that if a building is destroyed, the haunting is destroyed as well. This is not true. The energetic impression left on the area will remain even if the building is replaced. That is why you hear stories about ghosts walking through walls. Perhaps a doorway existed there at one time. The building that currently occupies this site is not the building in which this incident took place. That structure burned to the ground in 1788. In fact, none of the buildings that occupy this block today were here at the time. The French had built the city out of cypress, the only wood our indigenous termites did not eat. The homes were cottages with high ceilings, pitched roofs, and windows for cross ventilation.

The Eve of Good Friday that year, March 21, was a particularly windy evening. Shortly before midnight, Don Vincente Jose Nunez, the military treasurer for Louisiana, was praying in his personal chapel. Curtains billowing over the candles on his altar caught fire and within seconds the house was engulfed in flames. He barely escaped and ran down Chartres Street to the Plaza de Armas, called the Place d'Armes by the French and today known as Jackson Square.

Across from the Plaza de Armas sat a little wood church, the Church of St. Louis, where the St. Louis Cathedral sits today. He rushed into the church and asked the priests to ring the bells to alert the community of the fire. The priests refused. In the time it had taken him to reach the church, the clock had struck midnight and it was now Good Friday. It was forbidden to ring the bells on Good Friday for any reason. In addition, because it was such a windy night, the bells had been tied down to prevent them from accidentally ringing. Finally realizing the urgency of the situation, the priests began to untie the bells. Unfortunately, it was too late. The wind swiftly carried the fire through the colony. Nearly four-fifths of New Orleans was destroyed, 856 buildings in all. Many, many lives were lost that night.

Interestingly enough, the impression left on this area is not from any particular person who died that night. In fact, the impression left there is even not of what happened, but of what should have happened. The legend says that every Good Friday since 1788, shortly after midnight, bells can be heard inside these walls. The sound is very subtle, as if they are coming from a long, long way off. Those bells may not be traveling a physical distance, but they certainly are traveling a distance through time.

A local woman who once took some friends on our tour told me that she lived at 616 Royal Street. That building backs up to 617 Chartres Street. She invited us all to visit her courtyard, insisting that it was haunted. She reported hearing people there arguing in a foreign language in the middle of the night. As we entered the courtyard, I immediately felt a change in the energy. There was a certain heaviness to the area.

Our hostess pointed out one stairwell where that energy was very low. Entering the stairwell, I felt as though something *had* happened there. Over the next couple of days, I investigated the history of the building and the findings were astonishing! This building and the one next door stood on a site that had once been a very large estate. On December 8, 1794, children playing with fire near some hay started the second major fire that destroyed most of the city again. The two major fires in our city's history were started merely feet apart from another. Purely coincidental? Or could this area have been cursed as a sacred burial ground as warned of in earlier years?

The LaLaurie Mansion (1140 Royal Street)

*I*n 1834, a crime occurred that shocked our city beyond belief, a crime that eventually became known as the blemish on our city. Madame Delphine La-Laurie became an infamous name in New Orleans' dark history. She lived in the large gray mansion on the corner of Royal and Governor Nicholls Streets with her physician husband and her two daughters. They were socialites, best known for their lavish cocktail parties and their extremely well behaved slaves. This story came directly from the *New Orleans Bee*, the newspaper of the time.

While preparing for one of her parties, Madame LaLaurie was having her hair combed by a little twelve-year-old slave girl named Leah. When Leah accidentally pulled a tangle, Madame LaLaurie became enraged and she repeatedly beat the child with a bullwhip. Desperately trying to escape this brutal punishment, Leah ran out onto the balcony, climbed up onto the railing and fell to her death in the courtyard below. Madame LaLaurie was brought before the court, where she was fined a mere $300 for the crime. This was just one of several incidents where she had been brought into court for abusing her slaves.

A few months later, on April 10, 1834, a fire broke out in the LaLaurie home while one of their famous parties was in full swing. It is believed this fire was started by the slaves to bring attention to their plight. The fire brigade entered through the courtyard and proceeded to put out the fire in the kitchen, which was located in a separate building. The slaves then directed their attention to a locked room on the third floor.

Screams and cries could be heard from within the room. The firemen used a battering ram to break down the door and when it flew open, seasoned firemen fell to their knees vomiting from the stench of death within! Slaves were chained to the walls throughout, maimed and disfigured, obvious victims of cruel medical experiments.

Many were dead but some were still alive. Several had faces so disfigured they looked like gargoyles. One man looked as if he had been the victim of some crude sex change operation. One poor soul, a woman, had managed to break free from her shackles. Instead of being relieved that someone had come to rescue her, she ran in fear of further torture, jumping out of a window and falling to her death. The window remains sealed to this day. Another victim obviously had her arms amputated and her skin peeled off in a circular pattern, making her look like a human caterpillar. Yet another had been locked in a cage that the newspaper described as barely large enough to accommodate a medium size dog. Breaking the cage open, the rescuers found that all of her joints had been broken and reset them at odd angles so she resembled a human crab.

As the survivors were being removed from the residence a mob of the party guests assembled outside, outraged at what had obviously been going on within this house. They had no idea what kind of monsters the LaLauries were. Before the angry crowd could ransack the house and find them, Delphine and Louis LaLaurie and their children slipped out through the carriageway and disappeared at the river. Many believed that the LaLauries went back to Paris, but later evidence points to them possibly settling on the North shore of New Orleans near Mandeville. Immediately following this incident, the building became known as "the haunted house." Neighbors swore they heard screams and cries coming from within. Superstitious New Orleanians refused to walk on the same side of the street and many avoided the block completely. The house was vacant for decades.

Forty years later, the area was home to Italian immigrants. Families who lived in the house at that time told stories of seeing a large male covered in chains and blood walking the balcony. The children reported that a woman screaming in French was chasing them with a whip. One woman, a mother of twin babies, awoke in the middle of the night to find that a sock had been shoved into the mouth of one of the babies. Animals were found decapitated in the courtyard. It later was used as a furniture store. It had been open only a short time before the owner arrived one morning to find the entire inventory covered in urine, feces and blood. Believing he had been vandalized, he had the mess cleaned up and ordered new furniture. When he experienced the same thing a second time, he moved the business. One individual tried to open what was to be a haunted saloon, but locals refused to patronize the place. Again, it sat vacant.

Eventually the house was renovated into apartments as it is today. When floorboards were replaced in the slave quarters, the bodies of seventy-five people were found, some of whom had been buried alive! The screams and cries heard in the early weeks after the fire were real. Thinking these cries to be ghosts, no one even attempted to save these poor souls. To this day, this house is considered to be the most haunted in New Orleans. Several of our tour participants have fainted at this location. One man claimed that something chased him for a block and a half from this site. Another evening during our tour, the entire group's cameras failed to work only at the LaLaurie site.

Several years ago, a lady from St. Louis actually brought an entity home from this location. She experienced the usual signs of haunting: cold spots, electrical disturbances, etc. She also experienced a problem with her clocks all going to what she described as "military time." Research proved that during the LaLaurie era, what we refer to as military time would have been called European time. It took two months of helping her with house cleansing rituals to remove the entity. Once this woman's "symptoms" subsided, one of our company's pagers started displaying European time. Over the next four months, we exchanged the beeper for a new one three times. Each new pager would revert to military time. Eventually the entity moved on, probably returning to the property. One time, a tenant leaving his office on the first floor stopped to listen to the story. Afterwards, he approached our tour guide and reported that he constantly found the pictures had flown off the walls in his office and were scattered about the floor. He did not know the story and had no idea that the place was haunted. He has since moved from the building.

We had the opportunity to interview a family who had lived in the house in the 1970's. All the family members we interviewed confirmed that there were always strange noises in the house and that furniture would move about by itself. On dark and stormy nights the screams of a young girl could be heard ringing through the courtyard. One family member recalled a story about the man who rented behind the main house. There had been a particular door in his apartment that he never used. In fact, he had placed a coffee table in front of it. One night he was awakened from a deep sleep by someone opening that door. He was confronted by a man who stood above him looking down. Believing that he was dreaming, he ignored the man and went back to sleep. The next morning, he noticed that the table actually had been moved from the door. The house continues to be the most haunted in the city. Perhaps this intrigued actor Nicolas Cage enough to purchase the home in December, 2006.

Presence on the Balcony

Heavy ecto on LaLaurie Mansion

The Legend of Julie (732 Royal Street)

*I*n the 1700's & 1800's, the French aristocratic gentlemen in New Orleans engaged in a custom called plaçage, taking women of color as a mistress. Upon choosing a mistress, or "plaçee," the gentleman would provide housing for the young lady and care for her and any children they might have. The children carried the father's name and had the right of heirship.

Julie was one such plaçee. She had everything any woman could possibly desire, servants to wait on her, prepare her meals and draw her bath. But Julie wanted the one thing she could never have; she wanted to be her lover's wife. Even though society condoned and even encouraged plaçage, the law forbade interracial marriage.

Julie's lover knew that marriage was impossible. Even if he were to find someone in the city to marry them legally, the repercussions would be more than he could bear. His family would disown him, society would shun him and his associates would refuse to do business with him. He would lose his fortune and that was unacceptable.

But Julie wanted to defy the law and show everyone how strong their love was. She pleaded, she begged, she nagged for months. The constant fighting over marriage was destroying the peace of their home. After months of arguing with her over this issue, he offered her an ultimatum, so ridiculous, he believed, that she would surely ignore it. She would be forced to agree never to bring up marriage again and peace would be restored in their home.

One very cold, rainy night in December, as sleet pelted the city like bullets, he told Julie he would make her his bride in the morning if she would do just one thing to prove her love. She was to spend the entire night on the roof, not wearing a stitch of clothing. Before she had an opportunity to respond, there was a knock at the door. Some of his business associates had come to visit. Julie went up to the third floor. The men remained on the second floor, drinking, smoking cigars, discussing business and playing chess. They were so engrossed in their activities that they lost track of time. As the sun began to rise, Julie's lover escorted his guests to their carriages, bid them farewell and then proceeded to the third floor to be with Julie.

Entering the boudoir, he noticed that not only was the bed empty, it had not even been slept in. He felt an icy gust coming down the attic stairwell. As he raced up the stairs to the open window leading to the roof, he was struck with fear. This was no night for his love to be up on the roof. Even worse, if she had done it, he would be honor bound to marry her. He climbed out onto the icy slate roof, almost slipping and falling to his death. Once secure, he began to look around for Julie. He found her huddled by the side of the chimney. She was very cold, very wet and extremely dead.

Julie is the most predictable ghost in the city. It is guaranteed that she will appear one night out of the year, the coldest night in December. She is predictable but not modest, appearing totally nude. She still believes she will be a bride in the morning. But when the sun rises, Julie fades into the rooftop not to be seen on the roof for another year. The rest of the year, however, Julie is extremely active indoors. Until recently, the building where Julie once lived was home to the Bottom of the Cup Tearoom. The staff there once informed us that she is guaranteed to appear anytime her name is mentioned. She is the most active ghost in the city. She is also probably the most noted, as I heard about her when I was only eight years old. Her story continues to be told to schoolchildren as part of the city's legends. The Tearoom staff was graced with Julie's presence almost daily for many years. She was often heard laughing and sometimes crying throughout the building and several customers over the years witnessed the edge of her skirt whip around a corner.

A psychic named Otis, who worked at the Tearoom for 25 years, gazed into the courtyard pond and found the face of a young woman staring back at him. It seems that Julie loves attention. Psychic reports reveal that her lover was much older than she and very abusive. The psychics at the Tearoom did their own research on Julie and they believed she may have been pregnant at the time of her death. Julie has with her a cat whose presence has been experienced by a resident on the third floor. Julie takes every opportunity to get the attention she craves. When a documentary was filmed at the Tearoom several years ago, the owner of the building became aware of Julie's presence. As he spoke on camera, she walked around him running her hand across his back.

During our investigation, Julie performed lightheartedly for us. She seemed to prefer the reading rooms. One reader actually felt her on his neck as we interviewed him. He had goose bumps and the hair on his neck stood straight up. The water in his glass bubbled as if it had a life of its own. A photograph we took during the investigation captured Julie's silhouette leaning over his table. As Connie, a longtime Tearoom employee, spoke to us about Julie, her skirt began to rustle around as if dancing on its own. Connie exclaimed, "She's touching me! I can feel her." Connie and one of our staff felt Julie pass between them. As she walked by me she touched my right cheek.

Connie also told us of a temper tantrum, where Julie flung a box of paper clips across the room. Several days before our investigation, Julie turned on the intercom system allowing customers in the front to hear the consultations in the back of the shop. The readings on our monitoring equipment were extremely high. One of our own psychics involved with the investigations turned, stepping into Julie. She could feel the electrical impulses in her body.

She believed that Julie was fond of the colors light blue and lavender. She also felt that Julie did not wish to appear in photographs. Fortunately, we were able to capture a photograph of a misty, fog-like figure of an entity leaning down over one of the reader's tables at the Bottom of the Cup Tearoom. To the right of that figure sits a transparent image of a cat. Several weeks after our investigation, Connie informed us that she actually saw Julie in the shop. She followed her into a back room and when she cornered her, Julie vanished right before her eyes.

For the next couple of years, new stories about Julie's ghost emerged. During one of our investigations of the apartment above the tearoom, we were suddenly enveloped by the scent of magnolias, Julie's favorite flower. On another occasion, tour participants were making a purchase at the front counter when a coke can literally danced across the table. Recently, I purchased a book at the shop and when Connie attempted to check me out, her cash register suddenly began to ring up strange amounts and ignore the input of the correct amount. Once I acknowledged Julie, the correct amount totaled up for us.

During a visit to New Orleans, Kris Stephens, a photographer, visited the Bottom of the Cup on the off chance of capturing Julie on film. Kris was able to spend some time in the upstairs penthouse apartment and contacted me about her experience there. The activity in the apartment was high that evening. Kris saw Julie's skirt ruffle whisk around a corner and into a stairwell. Several times a woman's disembodied voice was heard calling out in French, "Henri" and "Henri en Rouge." At one point a door slammed shut as she called out his name. Kris also told me of some interesting photos that she had taken during her visit. When I met with her at the Bottom of the Cup, the staff informed us that Julie's presence had not been felt for several weeks. In her place however, a negative presence had turned up.

Philip and Jeanne, the son and daughter of the owner of the shop, had even been attacked by whatever was now haunting the shop. Each of them showed us scratches on their hands that had appeared just the day before. They each had three scratches on the top of their hands just below the third finger. Just days prior to the attack, a small but thick piece of glass flew across the room, hitting Jeanne in the back. There was no indication of anything broken to explain how that glass had suddenly appeared. Several employees reported feeling as if someone were poking them in the back. The two went on to tell me that renovations were going on in the courtyard, where another shop had just vacated a few months earlier. A section of a wall was being torn open and the workers had taken down the swing that Julie loved. I explained to them that often when renovations begin, it seems to disrupt the energetic flow of the spirits. It is not uncommon for ghosts to remain quiet and then become active once construction begins. Additionally, some of the furniture had been removed from the apartments and taken to other locations. There appeared to be a lot of change going on that could be attributed to the new malevolent spirit as well as Julie's lack of activity. I suggested to Philip and

Jeanne that they should put the swing back up and perhaps even return some of the furnishings to make Julie feel more comfortable again.

We were then led out to the courtyard to take additional photographs. There was a definite presence of something that, to say the least, was less than happy. When we returned to the shop, we were all overcome by the familiar and light presence of Julie. She was still there, but a bit low key, maybe somewhat sad.

The following day I looked through some old records on the building and interestingly enough found an old photo dated May 13, 1965. The sign on the front of the shop said, "Henri's Antiques." The building was purchased by Mr. Henry Weiss on May 29, 1962. The Bottom of the Cup later informed me that it was Mr. Weiss that had recently moved out of the building. We can only logically deduct that the ghosts are upset and angry that Mr. Weiss has left the building and they are acting out their emotions.

When spirits become attached to people, they can get rather irate when separated from them. I had a similar situation occur in my own house with my ghosts. I truly believe that I had so much trouble with my first book simply because the ghosts wished to be included in it and were overlooked. I was so involved in other properties that I failed to recognize what was happening in my own home, in the beginning at least. I later moved my computer downstairs and away from the portal. This caused activity to increase in my house similar to what was happening when I first wrote the book. I would hear my name being called throughout the house. My husband reported experiencing the same as well. One evening we came home from work and our kitchen light cover had been removed from the fixture and placed on the counter. The fluorescent light bulb was hanging from a wire and completely dislodged from its brackets. No one was home prior to our returning and finding this. I was also experiencing serious computer breakdowns. I eventually decided that it would be in everyone's best interest if I returned to work on the third floor office. This seemed to resolve the problems.

We were unable to determine who the negative entity was at the Bottom of the Cup. But we believe that whoever it was, this unhappy spirit had become unsettled by the renovations. Usually, such occurrences settle down once things get back to normal. And eventually, they did.

Kris did share with me some very impressive photographs. She was able to capture a large white image on the balcony of the penthouse apartment. Inside she had taken numerous photos, several of which were quite extraordinary.

In one photograph, a friend of Kris is standing with her back turned and the back of her head is seen. A piece of hair is being held straight out as if someone was standing there holding it, yet no one is there. In the background is a mirror. A portion of the woman's head is seen in the lower left corner of the mirror and above it, the image of a man's face. An enlargement of the mirror shows a heavy, bald man with a mustache. Another photograph of one of the rooms included a TV in the picture. An enlargement of the TV clearly shows a distorted face of what appears to be a man, just right of the flash reflected in the screen.

Woman's hair being held up, mirror in background

Close up face in mirror

Julie appearing over reading table

Face in TV

Madame LaBranche's Curse (700 Royal Street)

*T*he LaBranche House features the most photographed balcony in the French Quarter. In 1796, Monsieur Bienvenu gave this piece of land to Marianne Dubrevils, a free woman of color. At the time, it was opposite the public prison, where the Cabildo stands today. Covered with Creole cottages and outbuildings, the property was owned by four different women of color until 1835, when it was purchased by Jean Baptiste LaBranche. He built the present structure that year and, in 1838, commissioned the cast iron lacework. Unfortunately, he was killed in a duel a year before the work was completed, leaving the home to his wife.

Like many Frenchmen, Mr. LaBranche kept a plaçee, Melissa, in a different section of town. Apparently, this affair had not been hidden very well from his wife. Shortly after his death, Mrs. LaBranche invited the young woman to her home, where it is believed she drugged her with a cup of tainted tea. Once her rival was unconscious, the vengeful widow dragged her to the fourth floor attic and chained her to the wall. When Melissa woke up and found herself in chains, she began to stomp her feet, banging her wooden shoes against the floor so hard that she pounded them off of her feet. Melissa died in the attic of intense heat and lack of water. Mrs. LaBranche passed away several years later.

Duke University conducted an investigation and concluded that the ghosts of both Melissa and Mrs. LaBranche still occupy the house. Melissa appears barefoot, as she was when she died. She is a sweet young girl who is very mischievous. The site of her death, once an attic, was later used as an office. Employees there noticed her subtle gestures of gently moving about small objects.

Mrs. LaBranche was a greedy woman in her life, and a bitter ghost after her death. It has been reported that disturbances occur on the third floor whenever Melissa attempts to leave the confines of the attic. Cold spots are reported throughout the third and fourth floors and numerous orbs have been observed in photographs and video footage taken in the building.

Pirates Alley

*P*irates Alley is located in the French Quarter between the St. Louis Cathedral and the Cabildo. At one time, the area was a black market where pirates and privateers such as Jean Lafitte sold their goods. It was a virtual Mecca for any imaginable contraband: guns, liquor, women, slaves. Ironically, this trading place was situated between a Catholic Cathedral and what was once the seat of the Spanish Government. After the Americans took over in 1803, the Cabildo served as the Governor's mansion. Many a deal went sour in this alley. Sometimes, usually late at night, one can still hear distant voices speaking in French and Spanish. Sometimes there is an argument and even the distant sound of a pistol being shot.

Behind the Cathedral, next to Pirates Alley is St. Anthony's Garden. This is where the Creoles would duel with swords. Dueling was strictly for the sake of honor and the duels were usually only fought until one of the participants drew first blood. At that point honor was restored and the duel ended. It was only in very extreme instances that these duels would be fought until the death. In the wee hours of the morning, you can actually still hear the sound of metal hitting metal, swords clashing together in a duel. After 1803, the Americans chose to duel in City Park with pistols. Often these duels resulted in not just one but both parties dying for the sake of honor.

One of our tour guides, Midian, was walking through Pirates Alley toward Pirate's Alley Café after midnight on the night of a lunar eclipse. Suddenly, a man in pirate attire, carrying some kind of stick or sword above his head, darted out of a side alley. He ran ahead of Midian and then between him and the Cathedral. This is when Midian realized the figure appeared illuminated and he could see the iron bars and the foliage in the garden through it. The apparition continued down the alley and vanished, leaving nothing behind except the sound of footsteps echoing through Pirates Alley.

Many people have had similar experiences in the alley, especially near the café. Another one of our tour guides, Jerry Andersen, shared this story about a woman on one of his evening tours. When Jerry finished his story in Pirates Alley, the woman became aware that her watch was missing. She became frantic, almost crying, because it was a very expensive piece of jewelry with great sentimental value. The entire group searched throughout the area but the timepiece was nowhere to be found. It was concluded that the watch must have fallen off somewhere along the tour route, but the woman kept insisting that the clasp could not possibly open by itself. She continued the tour in shock and disbelief over the loss. After several more stories the group went into Pirate's Alley Café for their break. When the woman attempted to pay for her drink, she reached into her purse and was shocked to find her watch inside!

Pirate's Alley Café is New Orleans' only true European-style café and bar. Upon entering this historic building, you feel as if you have stepped back in time. Aleister Crowley, who practiced every conceivable kind of magic known to mankind, ventured to New Orleans from his native England in the early 1920's. Infamous for hanging in the local opium dens and absinthe houses, Crowley spent many hours in this café as he sipped his absinthe and wrote two of his books. Because witchcraft and magic were so clandestine during that era, the only documentation known to prove Crowley resided in the French Quarter are the magic books that he wrote in Pirates Alley. The bar continues to be the only one of its kind, an old European-style absinthe house.

Apparitions and celebrities alike have been seen in the café and neighboring alley, and many motion pictures filmed in New Orleans feature this location.

This is the alley Brad Pitt, who recently purchased a home on Governor Nicholls Street, walked through in the movie, "Interview with the Vampire." Cast members and crew frequently took breaks there. Patronage of the café by the cast and crew of this popular vampire movie spawned a decade of vampire life-stylers and enthusiasts to flock in homage to its sidewalk canopy covered tables. Celebrities such as David Keith, Peter Weller, Harry Anderson, and many others often are seen there as well.

Tour Guides Jonathan Weiss and Brent Baudean in pirate reenactment

"Backstreet Boy" Nick Carter and his brother Aaron
enjoying a private haunted tour with Kalila Smith

Actor Peter Weller with the Author and friends at Pirates Alley Cafe

Haunted History owner Sidney Smith with actor David Keith in Pirates Alley

The Singing Rain (Père Antoine Alley)

On November 23, 1762, in the Treaty of Fontainbleau, King Louis XV of France gave Louisiana to his cousin, King Charles III of Spain. The treaty was kept secret to all except the Spanish until March 5, 1766, almost four years later, when Don Antonio de Ulloa, our first Spanish Governor, arrived in New Orleans. The French Creole colonists were outraged; they wanted no part of Spanish rule. Six of these gentlemen organized an army and fought the first revolution in North America. Remarkably, they overtook the Spaniards and expelled them from the colony.

Spain was slow to respond. It was not until 1769 that another governor, an Irish expatriate named Don Alejandro O'Reilly, came to rule the colony. He was far better prepared. He brought with him an entire Spanish armada and easily took charge. Before long, he arrested the six leaders of the revolution and had them publicly executed. He then shocked everyone when he ordered their bodies were to be laid out in front of the Cathedral and set forth a proclamation that no one was to remove them for any reason. The corpses of these rebels were to remain in the hot New Orleans sun to rot, fester and decompose for all to see. The priest here at that time was a Capuchin monk named Père Dagobert. He was outraged by this act of terror and made numerous attempts to appeal to Governor O'Reilly. Each time he was turned away.

Finally, he took matters into his own hands. Very late one night, in the middle of a driving rainstorm, he gathered the families of those men. Together, they placed the bodies of their loved ones in coffins and Père Dagobert performed the Catholic funeral mass. He then led the funeral procession through what is now Père Antoine Alley up to what was then the St. Peter Street Cemetery, singing the Kyrie all the way there.

The impressions left that night by the strong emotions of Père Dagobert and the families of the slain men were not left in the church or even on the square.

These impressions, to which some refer as a miracle, were left in the rain. The legend says that if you go out through Père Antoine Alley and up Orleans Avenue in the middle of a rainy night, you will hear an unmistakable song. The closer it is to dawn and the closer you get to where the old St. Peter Street Cemetery once stood, the clearer and louder it becomes. It is the beautiful tenor voice of Père Dagobert singing the Kyrie.

Ghost at the Cathedral

The Ghosts of Shiloh (1113 Chartres Street)

One of the most famous historic figures to haunt our city is General P.G.T. Beauregard. He once lived in the home which is today the site of the Beau-regard-Keyes House Museum. General Beauregard ordered the firing of the first shot that started the Civil War. He also led men into the bloody Battle of Shiloh, where approximately 13,000 Union and 11,000 Confederate soldiers lost their lives. Some of these so-called men were boys as young as eleven or twelve years old. General Beauregard suffered intense grief and guilt due to the loss of life in that war, particularly in the Battle of Shiloh. Guilt is one of the strongest of human emotions.

It is believed that he continues to re-enact the scenes of a battle to this day inside the house. There have been many reports of the sound of gunfire, as well as screams and cries coming from within the walls. Inside sources reported to one of our guides that a mysterious mist has been seen in the main room of the museum. We were even told that often a bar that is used across one of the doors as a lock is found on the floor as though it had been thrown off.

The legend includes long-standing rumors of a paranormal report contain-ing the description of a battle ensuing in the main room of the museum. Guns and cannons are being fired. Men lie screaming, writhing in pain, their arms or legs blown off, and gaping holes in their bellies. The smell of smoke and gunpowder permeate the room. In the midst of this battle, an old gray-haired man in a tattered Confederate general's uniform walks about observ-ing the scene. He is uttering but one word over and over again. "Shiloh..., Shiloh..., Shiloh..."

We were once told a story by a young woman who had attended a party in the garden next to the house. She said that she had wandered into the main part of the museum, where she came face to face with a Confederate sol-dier!

It is commonly known that during the thirty years that Frances Parkinson Keyes owned this house she refused to live in it, preferring to entertain there only. Fearful of the ghosts, she allegedly lived in the slave quarters at the rear of the property. The ghost of chess champion Paul Morphy, born in this house in 1837, reputedly roams its rooms as well.

It is said that during the late 1970's, paranormal researchers verified that there are still other ghosts in this building, supposedly members of the Giancona family who later owned the property. The legend states that the family refused to give into the "Black Hand," otherwise known as the Mafia. When gunmen raided their home they defended themselves, killing all four of the intruders.

Ironically, after residing here for only six months, General Beauregard moved to a house in the 900 block of Royal Street, where he lived from 1867 to 1875. It was later sold to the Cangelosi family who, like the Gianconas, refused to give in to the "Black Hand." Mafia hit men went to the home early one evening and killed a child they believed to belong to the Cangelosi family. The child they killed, however, was that of a neighbor. That house is also said to be haunted.

The Sultan's Massacre (716 Dauphine Street)

One of the most mysterious ghosts in the French Quarter is that of a so-called "Sultan." He reportedly wanders the halls of the four-story house on the corner of Dauphine Street and Orleans Avenue. A *Times-Picayune* article written on February 11, 1979 recounts the Sultan's tale. There are discrepancies as to dates of the actual incident as well as to when the house was even built.

In the mid-19th century, Mr. LePrete, the owner of the house, was approached by a gentleman who introduced himself as an emissary working on behalf of a very wealthy Turkish Sultan. He said that his client was interested in renting this home and made a very generous offer. Since Mr. LePrete spent most of his time at his plantation in Plaquemines Parish and only used the French Quarter home during the opera season, he readily agreed.

It is said that the Sultan threw lavish, decadent parties and that the smell of opium and incense wafted out of the doors and windows at all hours. It is supposedly he who installed all of the ironwork on the entrances and windows, locking the house up like a fortress. He had a harem of beautiful women and young boys alike. An army of eunuchs was also on hand to protect the harem and the Sultan.

A neighborhood woman was strolling by the corner early one morning and noticed that for the first time in two years, the home was eerily quiet; no laughter, no music. She became aware of something dripping off the gallery and, looking up, realized that it was blood. She ran around to the front door, where she observed still more blood pooling from underneath. She reported the situation to the police who entered the property using a battering ram. Inside the house, they found that everyone had been slaughtered. Heads and body parts were flung across the rooms.

The Sultan turned out to have been an impostor, a brother of the real Sultan. He was found buried in the courtyard with so much soil in his throat it can only be assumed that he was buried alive in retribution for his treachery. It appears that a band of assassins sent by the real Sultan entered the home, defiled the harem and killed everyone. A gnarled, twisted tree once grew in the courtyard where the false Sultan was buried. It has since been removed.

According to the 1979 newspaper article, two women who had lived here during different periods said they had encountered the depraved imposter who had claimed to be a Sultan. Both women claimed to have seen his ghost. One woman moved out of the home after hearing shrieking, screams and gurgling sounds inside the house. To this day, residents report hearing body parts hitting the wood floors at night. Others say they have seen his robe whipping around a corner.

The Dungeon, a popular bar in the French Quarter, claims to have been the location where this "Sultan" kidnapped and tortured young girls into his harem. If you venture upstairs in the bar, located in the 700 block of Toulouse Street, there is a large poster-sized plaque giving the remainder of this bizarre tale. A restless entity is said to roam throughout the bar, sometimes even levitating the jukebox.

Reverend Zombie's Voodoo Shop
(723 St. Peter Street)

Our French Quarter Cemetery, French Quarter Ghosts and Legends, and Voodoo Tours all originate at Reverend Zombie's Voodoo Shop. The current structure was built by the American Homestead Company in 1918. The previous building, destroyed by fire in 1916, was the actual building where a most unpleasant incident took place. On September 19, 1788, Joseph Fernandez, a master carpenter, agreed to build a house for his brother, Andres. The house was to be built of brick with wood flooring and a shingle roof, and was to cost 4400 pesos. In true form to the old adage about hiring one's relative, the work was never completed. Andres later hired Francisco Gagnie, a Frenchman, to complete the construction. The original contract, which called for the house to be built of the finest materials, was written in French then translated to Spanish. On October 15, 1795, Fernandez filed suit against Gagnie claiming that he did not complete the work as agreed in the contract. After a great deal of litigation, on January 16, 1799, Gagnie was ordered to pay the disgruntled home owner the sum of 210 pesos and three reales, a large sum at that time.

Shortly after the judgment was ordered, Gagnie met with Fernandez at the property to explain that he was destitute and unable to pay such a large sum of money. Gagnie was never seen again after that meeting. In an investigative report of the Spanish Garrison, it was noted that the well at the rear of the property had been recently filled with brick and sand. That well was never reopened.

In the 1960's, the property had a very elaborate security system due to the owner's belief that someone cursing in French was constantly kicking his door in the middle of the night. Subsequent tenants of the rear slave quarter apartments have complained of missing construction tools. A current resident, Ms. Moller, has stated that she had left her hammer out one evening on the ledge of the old well. Although she was the only person on the property, it disappeared. In January 1999, on a very foggy night, she felt a cold, clammy hand grab her ankle as she sat on the ledge of the well. Draw your own conclusions!

Ecto at Rev. Zombie's Voodoo Shop

Legendary Haunts

Madame John's Legacy

*M*any ghost stories have survived throughout the years simply by word of mouth until they have become legends in our history. Some of these stories originated so long ago that it is impossible to exactly trace their origins. Where early records were destroyed in fires and hurricanes, we may have to depend on the ghosts themselves to tell their own stories. Sometimes their messages get confused and many remain a mystery.

There has been a building on the corner of St. Ann and Chartres Streets since 1720. The building that stands there today, however, is not the original structure. Parts of downstairs and most of the upper portion of the current building now house a restaurant called Muriel's. Some years ago, an employee of the restaurant reported that while she was preparing a table for service she was tapped on the shoulder. She turned around to find an attractive young man dressed in turn of the century clothing. He introduced himself as Joseph .

Peter expressed guilt and sorrow for having lost the property and then vanished. While investigating the history of the building, we found that it had once been owned by a Joseph Peter Lippardi. He had inherited it from his mother and then lost it through bad investments. His intense guilt has perhaps caused him to remain. He has been seen on numerous occasions, but only upstairs.

Part of the lower portion of the building is merely a large corridor with an adjacent entryway. It is believed that this area was at one time the site of a holding area for newly arrived slaves slated for auction at the exchange. Extreme sadness, anger, trauma and pain overwhelmed this space over a long period of time, leaving extremely strong impressions. The energy embedded here is so intense it cannot be removed or altered and the area is always cold. Many people feel a heaviness is the area, while others actually tune in to these tragic emotions and experience them. The longer one stays in the enclosure, the more noticeable the effects become. We brought the electromagnetic equipment into this building in January of 1998, and as soon as I turned on the meter the readings went wild.

At one time this same area was used to store building materials for the Cathedral. One of our guides recently had a tour group in this space and the entire group saw an apparition that appeared to be a young nun kneeling in prayer. She was described as being very two dimensional and possessing a slate gray color. It is likely that during the building of the cathedral, mass may have been celebrated in this space to bless the materials. The apparition may well be that of a nun present during one such mass. On yet another tour, a woman experienced a choking feeling in the building. She was apparently very sensitive to the energy there and literally began to gag. Since then, other tour participants have reported similar sensations.

Down the block from the Cathedral, the New Orleans Pharmacy Museum at 514 Chartres Street is housed in a building that once served as the office of Dr. Jay Dupas, a physician and pharmacist who operated a clinic here during the Civil War. Soldiers and officers alike would be kept in the clinic for observation or for surgery. Many of these men did not survive. The site today is still filled with the intense emotions of war. Visitors often report feeling weak or nauseous in the courtyard. The carriageway, once used as an entry for the clinic, has a constant stream of icy air in it. Often, those placing an arm into the carriageway have even felt tingling currents and the touch of an icy hand grabbing and pulling them.

Madame John's Legacy, located at 632 Dumaine Street, is another site where ghostly activity has been experienced but the cause is not known for sure.

From 1988 to 1994, during reconstruction of the Cabildo, Louisiana State Museum personnel were forced to temporarily set up offices in this location, also owned by the Museum. During this period of time, a number of ghostly disturbances were observed. On several occasions, a large mirror was seen literally levitating off of its hook and lowering to the floor entirely on its own accord. At a luncheon one day, a large, heavy silver coffee service rose off a table and moved across the room. At one time this house belonged to the family of René Beluche, a legendary pirate and swashbuckler. Although this ghost was never identified, some believe the ghost is either Beluche or possibly the first owner, Captain Jean Pascal, who was killed at Fort Rosalie in the 1729 Indian uprising.

One female ghost of legend is the Countess Charlotte. It is said that she was imprisoned in the Cabildo in the 1880's for murder. She escaped and after a brief taste of freedom was caught and returned to prison, where she committed suicide in her cell. This hostile, red-haired ghost continued to haunt the cell causing many subsequent inmates, mostly women, to commit suicide.

Another fiery female ghost haunting the French Quarter is known by many as the "Witch of the French Opera." She reportedly lived near the corner of St. Ann and Royal Streets and was in love with a much younger man who was not very faithful. After losing her love to a younger rival, she wrote him a tearful letter swearing revenge and then committed suicide. It is said that on the following night her ghost slithered into the apartment and turned the gas on, killing her unfaithful lover and his new love. For the next ten years, she was seen as a frightening figure dressed in white, with flowing hair and blazing red eyes. She would drift around the streets near the old French Opera and the rooming house where she once lived. One night a curious tenant found a tattered love letter behind a mantel and carelessly threw it into the fireplace. The letter burned and the ghost vanished, never to be seen again.

Numerous newspaper articles were written over the years about a certain house on Washington Avenue in uptown New Orleans. As early as the 1800's, it was said to have been haunted by a Countess who had previously lived there. Many a local of that era claimed to have heard the disembodied voice of a woman with a German accent. Not only that, her ghost is said to have frequented the socials held at the Pontchartrain Hotel as late as in the 1950's. The haunted house on Washington Avenue eventually fell into ruins and was torn down.

Some of the most historic legendary haunts are associated with the Battle of New Orleans. The infamous privateers Jean and Pierre Lafitte met with Andrew Jackson in the building located at 440 Chartres Street, now Pierre Maspero's Restaurant, to discuss strategy for the battle. The building is one of New Orleans' oldest and most historic, dating back to 1788 and originally used as a slave exchange. The restaurant workers here have reported excessive paranormal activity, particularly on the third floor. One waiter told us that he frequently senses a presence watching him from one particular corner in a room on that floor.

Tour guide and historian, René Laizier, told of an eerie tale of the haunted Chalmette Battlefield where the Battle of New Orleans took place.

"The final battle of the War of 1812 took place only a few miles down the river from New Orleans. When the news reached Andrew Jackson that the British had invaded Major Jacques Villere's plantation, waves of anger and fear reverberated through the entire city. The Louisiana Senate called for an immediate release of Jean Lafitte and his privateers who had been imprisoned just prior to Andrew Jackson's arrival. They believed, as did others, that the Baratarians, as they were called, were the only defense against the British. Jean Lafitte supplied Jackson with the necessary gunpowder and flint that was used to fight the war. Skirmishes took place over several months, with the final offensive on January 8, 1815. As morning arose and the fog that lay over the battlefield disappeared, the Americans found themselves staring at the greatest army in the world. The Americans were outnumbered two to one, yet victory was swift. In little over an hour, the Americans had triumphed. Over three thousand British soldiers were killed. American casualties amounted to seven dead and six injured. The lopsided victory occurred largely due to the effects of the cannons used to fight the British. Andrew Jackson cited that batteries three and four, served by the Baratarians, were especially brave in their service."

Tour guide René Laizier

While participating in reenactments of the Battle of New Orleans, René has experienced paranormal activity on the battlefield. He reported that on numerous occasions he has smelled black powder long before any of the reenactment cannons are fired. The strangest phenomenon noted on the field, however, is the growth of a particular thistle that is not native to the United States, and even more foreign in the swamplands of Louisiana. This thistle is native to Scotland only. The 3,000 soldiers who were killed on the battlefield on that cold January morning were the 93rd Scottish Highlanders. There is no scientific explanation for why or how the thistle grows on the battlefield. Yet it is worth observing that it is native to the home soil of the men who marched to their death on that day.

Not far from the battlefield is Jackson Barracks, where a sad ghost roams the armory. National Guardsmen stationed here have heard doors slamming, toilets flushing, and water running late at night. The ghost is believed to be that of 38-year-old Sergeant Henry Brunig, who shot and killed himself in the barracks. He had been the longtime caretaker and supply sergeant for the Washington Artillery, in charge of the horses that pulled the artillery wagons. In June of 1937, a veterinarian declared that twenty-one of the horses there were too old and unfit for military duty and ordered them destroyed. He had the remaining horses sent to other units and replaced them with motor vehicles. The following day, Brunig's lifeless body was found in the barracks warehouse.

Tour Guide Ernest Sylvester explaining burial procedures in St. Louis Cemetery #1

Tour Guide Renée Dodge speaking to a tour group

The Garden District

*T*he area of New Orleans between St. Charles Avenue and Magazine Street, from Jackson Avenue and Louisiana Avenue, is called the Garden District. By 1803, Louisiana had gone from being French to Spanish, then back to French. Napoleon was the ruler of France at this time. Although he vowed to the king of Spain never to give Louisiana to any other country except Spain, he never said he would not *sell* it to another country. It was this same year that he orchestrated the largest land for cash deal in history, the Louisiana Purchase. Although Spain had ruled for forty years, New Orleans had remained French and Catholic. French New Orleanians had no desire to become American. Most Americans at the time were Protestant, which did not settle well with these staunch Catholics. Additionally, New Orleanians had even less desire to have to learn English. From the mayor on down to all the citizens in New Orleans, there was an immediate rebellion against conforming to American rule that lasted for many years. It was because of this conflict that the city of Lafayette was founded. This area, now the Garden District of New Orleans, was the American section of Antebellum New Orleans. The Garden District rivals the French Quarter not only with its architectural majesty, but also with its rich history of civil uprising, creating numerous hauntings and legendary ghost stories.

The area began as a sugar cane plantation owned by the Livaudais family. In 1832, the plantation was sold by Mrs. Livaudais to a group of American investors through the city's first divorce settlement. The investors in turn divided the land into grids and sold them to wealthy Americans. These massive, ornate mansions were built to rival the beauty of the French Quarter, as well as to provide a way for upper echelon Americans to flaunt their wealth and status.

One of the oldest and most active ghosts in the Garden District is that of a small girl who died during the 1820's. Her family was visiting the plantation when she wandered off and became lost in the vast sugar cane field. Her small body was found after five days of an intense search. She had drowned in a pond on the property. To this day, she has been seen wandering through homes and yards throughout the area. The "lost child" is a legend in the Garden District.

At 2523 Prytania Street sits a stately mansion. It was once Our Mother of Perpetual Help Chapel. Anne Rice purchased it and then later sold the home to Buzz Harper. I conducted an investigation of the house and found that it is haunted by the benevolent ghost of a priest. Having been a chapel, it was also a rectory, where the priests lived. During the investigation, I was able to communicate with his spirit through a lamp in the bedroom where he had passed away. As I asked questions, one of the crystals hanging on the lamp would move in response. This priest had died of tuberculosis after spending years at the chapel. He continues to watch over the home as well as its inhabitants. Today the home is owned by actor Nicolas Cage.

The Buckner mansion was built in the late 1850's and is home to one of the more popular ghosts in the Garden District, Josephine. Josephine was a servant in the home who had remained with the family after slavery was abolished. She also acted as midwife and herbal healer in the community, giving way to rumors of her being a witch. It was common during that era for women to die in childbirth or babies to be stillborn, so many of the ghosts who inhabit the home in addition to Josephine are those of who died under such circumstances. It is not uncommon for lights to mysteriously go on and off on their own or chandeliers to sway back and forth with no apparent cause. An investigative team brought a psychic to the house that communicated with several spirits. Josephine responded by turning a light switch on and off.

The lavish home at 1331 First Street revealed a grisly secret that was discovered during renovations several years ago. When the current owners began the renovation, they found a small hollow area in one of the bedroom walls. When the wall was removed, a small room that had been sealed up many years before was revealed. The floors were rotted and in extreme need of replacement. As the floorboards were removed one by one, skeletal bones were revealed. Apparently someone had been buried under the floorboards and the room sealed up to conceal the burial. Oddly enough, the bones were placed in the form of skull and crossbones. The pelvic bones were used as the base in which the femur bones were arranged across the top in the shape of an X. The skull, with red hair still attached was placed at the top.

The owners of course contacted authorities and had the remains properly removed. No one knows whom the remains belong to or why they were buried in the house. There is no apparent ghostly activity in the house. So the "skeleton in the closet," so to speak, remains a mystery. Some suspect that slaves had done it in some sort of Voodoo ritual. The bones were those of someone who neither lived nor died in the house.

I noted similarities to some of the early Eastern European folklore regarding vampires. There were many ways that one could be predisposed to vampirism according to European folklore. But if predisposed, it was not during life, but after the death, that the family would take precautions against the dead returning as the undead. The skull had red hair. In many Eastern European countries, this was a sign of impending vampirism. If predisposed, upon death, often the family would decapitate the body, and arrange the bones in the shape of a cross, often putting the head near but detached making it impossible for the body to rise as a vampire. Perhaps no one will ever solve the mystery of the bones in the house on First Street. Meanwhile, speculation is all we have. Today the room is used as a nursery.

The elegant Greek Revival-Italianate house at 1239 First Street, with its rose-patterned fence and cast-iron balconies, is the former home of author Anne Rice. She used the house as the primary home of her fictitious Mayfair witches. A native New Orleanian, Rice purchased the home in 1989, using the funds from "Queen of the Damned" as her down payment. Reputed as haunted, she believed this house in particular "called out to her."

The first ghost is believed to be that of the original owner of the property, Alexander Hamilton Brevard. He invested his life savings in the home. Once it was completed, Brevard realized that he was unable to pay the taxes. The house was about to go into tax repossession. In an effort to render the home undesirable, he shot himself on the front steps with a 19th century pistol. The property went to his daughter who happened across some bonds that her father had apparently forgotten that he owned. She was able to pay the taxes and keep the house.

The other ghost is believed to be that of another previous owner, Pamela Starr. She had moved into the house at the age of 17 and died in the 1930's at the age of 92. She supposedly loved the house as much as Rice did. Throughout the years, many a ghost enthusiast has captured spirit phenomena on photographs both in and outside of the home. Most of the activity is seen on a gallery in front of the house, as well as the front garden and around a chair owned by Rice.

Ghost mist in Garden District trees

Haunted Hotels

The Omni Royal Orleans (621 St. Louis Street)

*T*his elegant hotel was built on the site of the old St. Louis Hotel, which once housed a bustling commodities exchange where all sorts of goods and property, including slaves, were auctioned off to eager purchasers. While it would seem likely that negative energy from such horrors would leave a strong residual haunting, the haunting documented here is a benign, active one. The ghost in this hotel is from an era later than the days of slavery.

When the St. Louis Hotel stood here, air conditioning and central heat were nonexistent. In the winter maids used gadgets called bed warmers to heat the beds before guests retired for the evening. A long-handled copper pan filled with hot coals would be placed under the covers and then the guest would be tucked in securely, ensured of warmth and comfort for the night. A ghostly maid is said to still provide at least a portion of this service to some guests from time to time. People staying here have told of waking up to find that the covers have been snugly fitted around the mattress as if someone had indeed tucked them in.

The Grand Palace (1732 Canal Street)

*T*he Grand Palace Hotel is located just outside of the French Quarter on the corner of South Claiborne Avenue. It was previously the Crescent Hotel, before that the Pallas Hotel, and before that, a retirement community known as the Claiborne Towers. Staff and visitors alike have experienced strange rides on the third elevator in the lobby. One desk clerk also described a "misty, dancing apparition" in the main ballroom. At one time when restoration had only completed through the eighth floor, upper portions of the building had lights flickering on and off late at night, although it is known that no one was up there.

Villa Convento Guest House (621 Ursulines Street)

A man taking one of our tours reported a visitation from an entity in room 120 of the Villa Convento Guest House. He told us that he and his girl-friend both experienced the feeling that they were not alone in their room. On their second evening in the guesthouse, he awakened in the middle of the night to find a woman sitting in a chair staring at him and then vanishing. The next night, he claimed to have had the same experience, only this time the apparition was that of a man. Although the manager of the guesthouse was unaware of any particular activity in that room, we were told that several guests have mentioned the sound of children laughing on the fourth floor where there was once an attic. This was not surprising because the guesthouse, built in the 1840's, was indeed a home for many years. There have also been unexplained electrical blackouts in room 209.

The Provincial (1024 Chartres Street)

*J*ust down the block from the Ursuline Convent sits the lovely Provincial Hotel. Building 5 of the hotel was used as a hospital during the Civil War. Maids report accidentally walking in on a Confederate soldier when they go to clean the rooms in this building. Some say that bloodstains appear and then disappear on the bedding in some rooms. Others report seeing ghostly surgeons making "sawing" motions as if they are amputating a limb! As far as we know, this is the only haunted area in this hotel. One employee said that one afternoon he had stepped out of the elevator in that building only to find that an entire section of the floor resembled an antiquated hospital operating room.

The Andrew Jackson (919 Royal Street)

*T*he Andrew Jackson Hotel was at one time the location for a boys' boarding school. The school was destroyed in the fire of 1794 and five little boys lost their lives. Children tend to make the strongest impressions of all on our plane. For many years, this hotel was primarily adults only, but still guests repeatedly called the front desk in the middle of the night to ask them to "keep the children quiet." The residual impression of the little boys playing in the courtyard can be heard throughout the night.

The Olivier House (828 Toulouse Street)

*T*his charming little hotel was built in 1836 by Madame Olivier, a wealthy plantation owner, for whom it is named. It was later owned by Elizabeth Duparc Locoul. There are countless stories about the ghost of a mysterious old woman dressed in black and carrying a rosary. She is said to roam the property cursing at staff and visitors alike. The ghost appears to be that of Madame Locoul.

Elizabeth Duparc Locoul reputedly had a nasty disposition. It was said that she went as far as to have her servants branded to prove that they were hers. Those who knew her said she was spiteful, vicious and hateful. A relative once described her as so mean she probably would not even give her baby teeth to the tooth fairy. Indeed, after her death, her baby teeth were found among her belongings.

She always dressed in black and was never seen without her rosary. It is said that she would wander throughout the house and the courtyard mumbling her rosary to herself and that she would scream and curse at anyone who interrupted her prayers. Most of the activity is located in the first room in the building where it is believed that Elizabeth died in 1884, at the age of 88.

I stopped in one evening just to introduce myself and asked if I could investigate the property. The management was so friendly and helpful that they invited me to go into the room since it was unoccupied. As soon as I entered, I could smell the unmistakable odor of an elderly person who had recently died. I immediately picked up that whoever died in the room was an aged, sickly, female. The air was very thin as if at a high altitude even though the room is on the first floor. I began to feel lightheaded, dizzy, and a bit nauseous. There was a distinct coldness in the area directly over the bed and an indentation in the mattress as if someone was seated there.

As I held my hands over the area for several minutes, pain shot deep into my arms and I began to feel the physical pain of an old woman who had been ill for a very long time. I believe she suffered from arthritis in her joints. I picked up on her emotions as well. I am convinced that she dreaded death so much that she is too afraid to cross over and therefore stays attached to this room. She was aggressive toward people in her life because she was so unhealthy and pain stricken. She is a malevolent spirit today only because of her fear. A strict Catholic, she continues to pray the rosary in the overwhelming trepidation that she will go to hell.

I left the room after only a few minutes because I was feeling more indisposed by the moment. I thanked the desk clerk and left the guesthouse. The dizzy, sick feeling persisted for at least half an hour afterwards. In fact, I was so disoriented that I lost all sense of direction and began walking south on St. Peter Street, all the while believing myself to be walking east on Burgundy Street.

The Olivier House
(828 Toulouse Street)

The Place d'Armes Hotel (625 St. Ann Street)

The Andrew Jackson Hotel
(919 Royal Street)

The Place d' Armes (625 St. Ann Street)

*T*his story was originally told by one of our tour guests who shared with us her strange experience at Place d'Armes Hotel. She said that one evening she was on her balcony enjoying the sunset and chatting with the person she believed to be staying in the room next door, a man that she simply described as the "bearded gentleman."

After their brief conversation she returned to her room. She had found him to be so intriguing that later in the evening she inquired about him at the front desk. The desk clerk informed her that the room adjacent to hers was not occupied at that time. She insisted that it was and began to describe the man. The desk clerk replied, "Oh, him, that's our ghost!" She thought, of course, that he was pulling her leg. We checked the next day with one of the desk clerks and indeed he told us that many people had experienced a visit from this bearded gentleman. The Place d'Armes Hotel was the location of the first school in Louisiana and he is believed to have been its first headmaster, who died in the fire of 1788.

A week or so later, we received a call from this woman. While she was in town, she purchased a hat. She showed the hat to one of her traveling companions who photographed her in their room modeling it. When she had the film processed, who do you think was reflected in the mirror behind her in the photograph? You guessed it... the bearded gentleman!

In April of 1997, my husband and I stayed at the Place d'Armes on our honeymoon. When we checked in, the desk clerk recognized us and to tell us many other strange stories about the hotel. After the school burned down, the space was later rebuilt by the Spanish and used as a prison, with gallows in the back.

He also told us that a couple of months before our visit the fifth floor had been renovated. During the renovations, the electricity and phones were turned off on that floor. One evening about 2:00 a.m., his switchboard rang eight times. It lit up 501,502,503,504,505,506,507,508. Each room on the fifth floor rang down to him even though those rooms had no working phone lines at that time! We of course insisted that our second night there we stay in a room on the 5th floor. After all, the only ghostly activity in the downstairs suite had been the TV coming on by itself about 4:00 a.m.

During our stay on the fifth floor, we had a number of strange experiences. The first took place in the elevator. Regardless of what button we pressed, the elevator always stopped on the second floor. In our room, the shower door opened and closed by itself. And at 2:00 a.m. the telephone repeatedly rang with nobody on the other end. Needless to say, the desk clerk verified that the switchboard had not rung for hours.

There were a great number of disturbances in the parking garage the week that we stayed at the Place d'Armes. Attendants reported lights going on and off and horns blowing without any explanation. Several employees reported that they felt strange energy in the garage at night. We investigated the ground floor of the garage. One photo we took of the elevator door shows a fog around the door and the image of a man standing in front of the elevator, as if waiting for it to open. Another clearly shows the face of what appears to be a large man with a full beard looking down from the ceiling in the garage. He seems to be wearing what looks like a pirate's hat.

Another story told to us by the front desk clerk may be the strangest of all. A couple staying on the second floor were awakened about 3:00 a.m. by light coming in through an open door. A little girl who appeared to be about six or seven years old was standing in the doorway crying. When they turned the light on, they could see that the door was not only closed but the deadbolt locked. There was no little girl. Nevertheless, they called the desk clerk and reported a lost child. When the desk clerk told them that there were no children in the hotel they became furious. They left in the middle of the night.

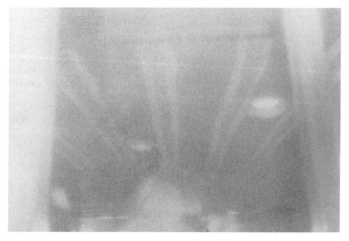

Ghost in Place d' Armes garage

The Pontchartrain (2031 St. Charles Avenue)

*T*he Pontchartrain Hotel was once a residential hotel for affluent senior citizens. I had the pleasure of interviewing Douglas Leman who had worked there for 47 years. He is a charming man who began his employment there in 1952 as a busboy, and in a short time, worked his way up to Maitre d'. He told me that in that day there were 35 permanent residents in the hotel and described this time as a grand era.

Two of the most colorful residents in the building were widowed sisters who resided in a suite on the ninth floor. They were always dressed impeccably and were often seen riding in the back seat of their black, chauffeur-driven Lincoln. After the sisters died, the housekeeping staff reported that the women were still appearing in their suite and in the corridor. To this day, guests report hearing disembodied voices of women late at night on that floor.

Back then the Pontchartrain was the venue of almost nightly parties. The residents all knew each other and enjoyed socializing regularly. One of the guests Mr. Leman vividly remembered was a woman known to most as the Countess Carpania. As the story goes, she was an American who visited Italy where she met the Count Carpania. She married him and remained in Italy until his death. She then returned to New Orleans and kept her title for the rest of her life. Mr. Leman recalled that when she would enter the Caribbean Room, she would present her hand to him and he would be obliged to kiss it. He said that although she was not a resident of the hotel, she frequented the socials held there.

Mr. Leman recalled a resident he referred to as "Mr. B." He described Mr. B. as a socially prominent, yet mysterious, gentleman who moved into the hotel following a divorce. He attended all of the social functions, but only briefly. He would stay long enough to flirt with the women in the room and then depart into the night, not returning until the early morning hours. He may have simply been a "night person," but what Mr. Leman found odd about this individual was that he never ate at these socials. Mr. B. would say, "Now Douglas, you know I won't be staying for dinner," and would leave right about the time the sky began to grow dark. Mr. Leman confided in me that he suspected that this gentleman was a vampire, although that can hardly be proved.

The Prytania Inn (2127 Prytainia Street)

Room 9 of the Prytania Inn is often used for Halloween parties. It is believed to be haunted by the ghost of a young child they call Isabel, who suffered a fatal fall down the stairs many years ago. She is a benevolent spirit who continues to play in the room.

St. Vincent Guest House (1507 Magazine Street)

Details provided by an employee here explained why the attic of this particular hotel was so cold and bleak. The building once housed Civil War prisoners and was later an orphanage. Unruly children were sometimes locked in the attic, compelled to kneel and do penance in the very location of where prisoners of war had been chained. There is a strong residual presence of this oppressive energy in the attic.

The Bourbon Orleans (717 Orleans Avenue)

The Bourbon Orleans Hotel was originally two separate buildings, the Grand Ballroom and the Orleans Theatre, built in 1817. The left staircase is the original staircase to the ballroom, and the right staircase was added in 1966. The ballroom today is only a portion of the original Grand Ballroom. These buildings were among the most historic structures in the entire Southeast, and were the venue of some of the area's major social events. The buildings were designed to allow patrons of the theatre to flow out into the ballroom to attend soirees after the show. That ballroom is where Andrew Jackson announced his candidacy for the presidency. It was also the setting for the Quadroon balls, where Mulatto mothers would take their Quadroon daughters to be presented to society hoping to place them as mistresses of wealthy Frenchmen.

Later, when the ballroom was used as a gambling house, it was the only place in the city where these gentlemen could bring their mistresses out to socialize. Many a duel was fought over the hand of a young lady or because of a gambling quarrel in St. Anthony's Garden just down the street behind the Cathedral.

In 1870 the theatre became a courthouse. Shortly thereafter, both buildings became a convent for the Sisters of the Holy Family, a group of African American nuns that ran an orphanage for children of color. Here they remained for 80 years. In 1963, the management of the Bourbon Orleans made the nuns an offer they couldn't refuse, and moved them out of the French Quarter to a more appropriate location. It has been one of the finest hotels in the city ever since, a very haunted hotel at that.

One of our favorite stories about the ghosts here is about a worker who was hammering in one of the stairways. He accidentally hit his thumb with the hammer and yelled out an obscene word. He was immediately slapped in his face! When he noticed that there was no one there, he ran away screaming, never to return, not even for his last paycheck.

One prevalent ghost haunting in the ballroom is a suave young man who enjoys entertaining the ladies. Besides fluttering the curtain or spinning the crystals on the chandeliers, he has been known to sneak up behind women and kiss or caress them lightly on the neck. Incidentally, he prefers blondes. Many of the ghosts here are children. On the fifth floor, guests frequently see a little blonde girl chasing a ball. In fact, for a while in 1997, catering was suspended on that floor because the head of room service kept hearing a disembodied voice calling her name. On the sixth floor, guests frequently have been startled by water faucets suddenly going on by themselves.

The seventh floor is home to an older gentleman, a very benign spirit. He wears a Confederate uniform and carries a rifle. During our investigation, we photographed the room where this entity appeared. He appeared in the photograph as nothing more than a misty haze surrounded by bright light. A mysterious young woman also resides there, usually in the Gabrielle room. She is often seen at the window gazing down at the pool area. Although not at all malevolent, she is very aloof and has a strange aura about her.

Some time ago, one of our tour guides celebrated her wedding reception in one of the rooms on the seventh floor. While she was seated, she felt the presence of a child come over and sit on her lap. Many people experience one hand going cold as a tiny ghostly hand slips into theirs. A gentleman on our tour one evening told us that he had been employed as a doorman at the hotel many years ago. He said often late at night he would fall asleep at the desk, only to be awakened by the voice and a nudge of a child. When he opened his eyes, no one would be there.

When I investigated this hotel, the meter recorded large amounts of energy in the ballroom. Just as I would snap my camera, the energy would move away. I followed this mischievous spirit all around the ballroom. I could even see the curtains flutter lightly, and then remain still. There is no indication that any of the ghosts in this hotel are malevolent.

Tour guide Bill Arendell in the haunted ballroom of the Bourbon Orleans Hotel

The 1891 Castle Inn Bed & Breakfast (1539 4th Street)

*I*n the quiet splendor of the Garden District, guarded by gargoyles, sits a large stone mansion called the 1891 Castle Inn, a popular bed & breakfast. It is appropriately named, decorated in lavish antiques including several standing suits of armor.

The owner had reported numerous experiences in the house and invited me to do an investigation. Their ghosts were definitely active. On one occasion, an employee heard a man cough in one of the empty rooms. Guests have reported seeing spheres of light moving about the third floor of the house as well as hearing voices. One ghost is quite a prankster, sometimes taking keys of visitors and moving them to obscure places.

Once acquainted with the house, I was left alone. One room was distinctively colder than the rest, so I set up a digital recorder and left it in there. I then explored the house, taking photographs, hoping to capture something on film. Unfortunately, I was not successful with photographs.

Still, there was notable activity. In room 5, I experienced a very strange, almost suffocating, heaviness in my chest. The most activity was found in a room on the third floor called the Bordello Room. Earlier in the evening, I had felt compelled to leave a recorder in this particular room. I later found distinct EVP on this recorder. The voice was not clear enough to distinguish what was being said, but it was a voice nonetheless. When I retrieved the recorder from the room, something prompted me to look up. The chains hanging from the ceiling fan were swaying back and forth rapidly. Someone was unmistakably there.

As I began to speak to the presence, I felt as if I was embraced by cold air. I could feel the spirit touching my cheek. I sensed that this was a male entity, probably in his 50's or 60's. I set up my communication board and proceeded to ask questions. I asked the entity to spell out his name. The board spelled out U-N-C-L-E T-I-M. The spirit then indicated that he had been in his 60's when he crossed over. He also communicated that he was not the only entity present on the property. He spelled out another name, C-H-A-R-L-E-S. Charles was described by the spirit as a man in his 40's. The spirit then spelled out F-R-E-D-E-R-I-C-K. He described this spirit as that of an infant. The spirit then directed the disk on the board to GOODBYE. This meant he didn't care to communicate any further. The presence of these spirits made me feel very comfortable. I spent an extremely peaceful rest of the night in The Castle Inn that evening.

About two weeks later, I began to work on a project with the MTV series, "Fear." A friend, Kris Stephens, had been doing some research with the series and directed them to me during a shoot in New Orleans. She also mentioned that through the show she had met an extraordinary young woman named Melanie, who was very gifted. Kris described her as "one of the clearest channels" she had ever met. Coincidentally, Melanie and her boyfriend were planning a trip to New Orleans that week. When Melanie contacted me about meeting and taking some of our tours, I told her about the Castle Inn and she booked a room there for the following night.

That evening, Melanie and her boyfriend constructed their own message board for communication. I did not give her any information regarding what I had found on my previous investigation. The next morning, we compared her responses to mine. The one thing we had in common was that she too had the name Charles spelled out on the board. She had two other names given to her as well, Jim and Henry. The spirits told Melanie that Jim was the son of Charles. Jim was of mixed heritage, Haitian, French and English.

This made a lot of sense to me. Before the Garden District was built, the space where the Castle Inn sits and numerous blocks surrounding it had been a plantation. Charles, being of French descent, would most likely have had a mistress, probably a slave on the plantation. It was not uncommon for these men to keep women of color as mistresses, but to father their children as well. Usually, this meant that the children were half Haitian.

The spirits did not identify who Henry might have been, only that he died in room 5, the room where I experienced the pressure in my chest. Melanie also felt that at some point in time, a suicide had taken place in room 11.

The following day, I again met with Melanie at the Castle Inn. We went over her experiences from the night before, and she once again began to channel. The spirits coming through her were very clear to me. Melanie led me to the basement where the spirits told us about a murder having occurred some time before the house had been built. She put her hands to her throat as if she was choking. Immediately, I sensed that there had been a hanging.

She then ran around to the front of the house and began to point at a gas lamp. "Light?" I asked. "No, fire," she replied. There had been a fire on the ground. She kept making circles on the ground with her hand. Circles and fire made me suddenly think of a Voodoo ritual. The spirits confirmed that the slaves on the plantation had practiced Voodoo there. One of them must have been hanged there. The spirits led us to believe that it was possibly Jim, the son of the plantation owner.

Further documentation indicated that seven deaths occurred in the house throughout the years, mostly due to yellow fever. Other research on the property proved that there was once a light skinned black man named "Henri" who resided on the property, no doubt Melanie's "Henry." He was a paid servant during the late 1890's, a butler and driver for the family who resided there at the time. Henri was fond of cigars, liquor, and ladies. It is believed that he died in a drunken stupor when a lit cigar set his bed afire. Guests sometimes sense the faint aroma of cigar smoke. Henri has also been known to stroke the hair or caress the skin of attractive female guests.

This location seems to be a favorite place for the ghost of the little lost girl of the Garden District. The apparition of a small girl in a white dress has been reported often throughout the house. She is usually barefoot, wandering to and fro as if searching for something. Perhaps to her, she is still in the field of sugarcane looking for a way out.

Guests and employees alike report objects moving about on their own, lights and appliances turning on and off, unexplained sounds, including footsteps, water faucets turning on and off in empty bathrooms, and brief glimpses of a man's apparition throughout the property.

Tour guide Rene Laizier in the Vampire's Lair Suite

Magnolia Mansion, photograph by Fred Plunkett

Photos courtesy of Magnolia Mansion

Magnolia Mansion (2127 Prytania Street)

*T*his Greek revival mansion, one of the most magnificent in the entire Garden District, was built in 1857 by Alexander Harris for his beloved wife, Lizzie. In 1869, Mr. Harris died in one of the many yellow fever epidemics that ravaged the City of New Orleans. Doctors of the time had no knowledge of tropical medicine and had no idea that mosquitoes breeding in water carried this volatile disease. Yellow fever attacks the liver, and its victims become jaundiced and run high temperatures until they vomit blood and a black grainy substance, fall into a coma and die. Those lucky enough to survive the disease become immune to it. Because the disease was so uncontrollable, those who suffered from it were quarantined in their homes, where most of them died. This could certainly explain why his spirit frequents Magnolia Mansion.

Ten years later, his widow sold the property to a Mr. Maginnis. On July 4, 1889, a major hurricane hit the Gulf Coast area. Mr. Maginnis was staying there at the time, and he was killed by a bolt of lightning while attempting to free a tree branch from his roof. His funeral was held in his New Orleans home, now known as Magnolia Mansion. During thunderstorms, the sounds of his footsteps can be heard walking on the roof. Every 4th of July weekend, Magnolia Mansion experiences a predictable temporary blackout, due to unkown causes.

His daughter, Josephine Maginnis, co-founded the New Orleans Chapter of the American Red Cross which used the home as a headquarters from 1939 to 1954. Even today, some guests report feeling someone "tucking them into bed" at night or the sensation of someone sitting on the bed. Others say they have felt someone holding their hand or watching over them. Late at night, people have heard footsteps in the upstairs hall, an old pocket watch opening and closing, and even the sound of an old fashioned music box. Although Magnolia Mansion does not allow children as overnight guests, on more than one occasion the handprint of a small child has been found on the bathroom rugs. Numerous guests taking photographs both inside and outside have captured images of ghosts. Fortunately, all the spirits who dwell in the mansion appear to be friendly and visitors who stay here find their ghostly presence pleasurable and strangely comforting.

During a recent renovation, the owner returned from an errand to find the entire crew seemingly taking it easy. When she asked why they were not working, they directed her to the dining room, parlors and grand hallway. All these walls appeared wet as if a water pipe had broken or a fresh coat of gloss paint was oozing down onto the floors, yet neither was the case. There being no other logical explanation, the owner concluded that it must be ectoplasm.

She spoke to the house and its spirits. Reassuring them that she was trying to restore it to its formal beauty and glory, she told them that they were more than welcome to stay as long as they did not harm or destroy the mansion, and as long as they did not hurt or scare her employees or her guests. She did, however, give them permission to frighten the wits out of anyone who entered the mansion with ill intent. She then said the Lord's Prayer and cleaned the ectoplasm off walls and floors. The workers had flat out refused to do it and said they would not be back to work until it was gone. In fact, many of them left that day never to return.

On at least two other occasions, it was clear that the spirits had heard the owner's prayer and were keeping up their end of the bargain. One day when she was alone in the house with the live-in caretaker, she heard him frantically calling to her to come to the dining room. There she found him frozen by fear beneath a violently shaking chandelier. When she repeated her invocation to the mansion and said the Lord's Prayer, the chandelier immediately stopped shaking. Sensing that it was time for the caretaker to leave, she terminated his employment and sent him away, confident that the spirits had protected both her and the mansion.

The next caretaker was on the telephone in the dining room one day when the 300-pound cypress kitchen door suddenly opened and slammed shut all by itself. A cold wind rushed past him and scared him out of the house. It turned out that neither of these men was up to any good.

One of the owner's favorite experiences in Magnolia Mansion involved a couple who celebrated their honeymoon there. Shortly after their arrival, the husband called in a panic saying that his wife was not feeling well. The owner arranged for a taxi to take them to nearby Touro Infirmary. Returning during breakfast the next morning, the couple reported that at the hospital they found out the bride was pregnant and that the doctor there ordered her to have complete bed rest for at least one day. Exhausted, they both lay down for a nap in their room named "The Vampire's Lair." The bride, who was running a fever, left her covers off.

Thinking she felt her husband pull the sheets over her, brushing her cheek, she opened her eyes to look at him and say "thank you, I love you," only to find him sound asleep on his side, facing away from her. She thought this to be a sweet and caring gesture and was not scared by it. This was the first report of the mansion's resident spirit maid from the top floor coming downstairs to care for someone in need. Who she is remains unknown, but it is believed that in her lifetime she cared for the sick, the elderly and children.

When asked if Magnolia Mansion is haunted, the owner tells guests, "You will have to tell us when you leave. Although we have friendly hosts and ghosts, the ghosts don't come with a guarantee."

Antonio Banderas with Sidney Smith, after re-visiting sites from the movie *Interview with a Vampire*.

Lafitte Guest House (1003 Bourbon Street)

*H*otel personnel at this property informed us that room 21 was haunted by the ghost of a mother still grieving the loss of her two daughters. Both girls died in room 21. The younger daughter, Marie, died during one of the yellow fever epidemics that took the lives of thousands of children in colonial New Orleans. After losing little Marie, her mother refused to leave the room. Adding to her grief, an older daughter, Evangeline, is believed to have committed suicide in the same room where their mother was now bedridden.

When I interviewed the owner of the guesthouse, Andy Crocchiolo, he provided me with a genealogy of the family along with a 1989 report from a psychic who investigated the activity here. This psychic induced a trance state and utilized channeling and automatic writing to recount the tragic story of this mother's tortured soul. The psychic heard the sounds of horses' hooves clapping against the street as she had a vision of woman dressed in a green, satin hoop skirt, her small feet crammed into pointed shoes. The woman, whom she called "Madame," has dark hair pulled tightly into a bun. She is seated near the fireplace, fanning herself with a lace fan. Speaking in French, the spirit tells her that she is having everything burned, but begs to be allowed to stay in the room. Describing a tiny black coffin and a funeral for her child, she says she is far too grief-stricken to attend.

As bells tolled, the chandelier in the room flickered twice. Madame's words are the essence of anguish and despair. "We live only to die. Only for a time can we have our little ones, I want to stay in the room, then I don't have to go out and face those who wait for me at the church. Holy Mary, save me from all of my sorrow, Mother of Mercy. Just let me rock my little one again. Don't let me leave the room. They wait for me with the little casket covered in flowers." The session lasted thirty minutes, and then Madame disappeared. Hotel staff also report seeing an apparition of little Marie throughout the building.

In 1965, Mr. Crocchiolo was planning a cruise in the Caribbean. The day he had planned to leave, he walked past the fireplace in the parlor to see that the words "no voyage" had been sketched into the ashes. The ashes then blew around onto the floor. As he cleaned the mess, he became overwhelmed by the stench. Later that week, Hurricane Betsy entered the Gulf of Mexico, eventually striking New Orleans head on. Had he taken that cruise, he would have been stranded and unable to return to the city to prepare his property for the storm. Hurricane Betsy was one of the most devastating hurricanes to hit New Orleans, rivaling the damages caused by Katrina of 2005.

This was not the only time the ghost rescued him from harm. He was carrying a stack of towels down the stairs when he lost his balance and began to stumble down the long, steep staircase. He swears that something unseen caught him, breaking his fall and perhaps saving his life.

Guests staying here have captured the image of a little girl in the mirror of the hallway, right outside of room 21. Others have heard the laughter of small child late at night in the same hallway.

The Ashley House (2111 St. Charles Avenue)

*T*his antebellum raised cottage was built in 1841, making it one of the oldest in the historic Garden District. It is also one of the most haunted. Its raised construction was intended to protect the owners, who held the superstitious belief that yellow fever and malaria came from the ground.

During the Civil War, it was used as an infirmary and also housed prisoners of war. While it is believed that the majority of ghosts here are those of soldiers, prisoners and injured alike who occupied the house used the lead from bullets to etch their memoirs onto the walls. These writings were authenticated in 1983 by Wilbur E. Meneray, Ph.D., head of the Rare Books and Manuscripts Collection of Tulane University. The hotel has preserved many of the writings behind plexiglass. Meter readings were at their highest level throughout the property and remained there for the duration of our investigation.

A tragic story from the days before the Civil War also shadows this historic building. A distraught slave, who had been taken on as a mistress by her widower master, murdered his children. Suddenly filled with remorse, she took her own depraved life. Visitors have heard the sounds of a piano playing and children laughing. Many have reported the feeling of being watched from the antique photographs. We concluded that this location has perhaps the highest concentration of paranormal activity in the area.

Lafitte's Blacksmith Shop

Ghosts in Lafitte's courtyard

Spirited Spirits

Lafitte's Blacksmith Shop (941 Bourbon Street)

*L*afitte's Blacksmith Shop, according to the plaque on the door, was built in the 1720's, is the oldest working bar in the country and is the second oldest building in New Orleans. The property is believed to have been used by Jean and Pierre Lafitte as a New Orleans base for their Barataria smuggling operation, based on the fact that around that time the property was owned by the family of Simon Duroche and privateer, Rene Beluche. Beluche was Captain of a legendary ship named "Spy." Jean Lafitte has been described as a privateer, an entrepreneur, a diplomat, a spy and a hero in the Battle of New Orleans. He aided General Andrew Jackson in defeating the British at Chalmette Battlefield in 1815.

Today, this bar is considered to be one of the most haunted in New Orleans. The ghosts of soldiers and pirates alike have been seen walking about the building in the middle of the night. One familiar apparition is that of a woman with long dark hair who is dressed in black. She has made appearances in the bar late at night as well as in the upstairs office. There are no records to document who she might be, but one can surmise there was no shortage of women in the company of pirates. This one, for whatever reason, has chosen to stay here. The candlelit ambiance of Lafitte's has also given it a reputation for being a vampire tavern.

The Bombay Room
(Inside the Prince Conti Hotel, 830 Conti Street)

*T*his property was once a coffin factory and later became a public bath-house for over fifty years. When we investigated the Bombay Room, a bartender gave an account of the activity he had been experiencing. He stated that the energy was most prevalent in the kitchen area, particularly the dishwasher. He reported that the machine seemed to "have a mind of its own." It would turn itself on at odd times when it was not supposed to and it would not turn on when it was supposed to. He said the activity increased and decreased depending on who was around at the time. There is an active haunting in Prince Conti Hotel itself as well. One of the desk clerks reported that the ghost of a Storyville Madame who died in one of the rooms still haunts the hotel. It is possible that this ghost wanders in and out of the bar and the kitchen as well, which would explain the occurrences there.

Cosimo's (1201 Burgundy Street)

*I*n the early 1960's, this quiet, secluded bar in the residential section of the French Quarter was the supposed meeting place of individuals connected with the JFK assassination conspiracy. These individuals were later identified during District Attorney Jim Garrison's investigation. Late at night, ghostly apparitions still appear at the tables in the back room and fragmented whispers of an assassination plot are heard.

The ghost of a woman dressed in a robe and slippers has also been seen through the years wandering in the bar. She is believed to be the ghost of the mother of the current owner of the building. The family once used the building as their home, and the bartenders claim she is still present.

A male entity frequents this bar as well. The bartenders call him "Uncle Joe." He always sits in the same seat, the one on the far end near the front. He is said to be dressed formally, in top hat and tails. I interviewed one bartender who said that the members of the staff leave drinks out for Uncle Joe. Some researchers theorize that many entities remain earthbound due to addictions acquired during their lifetime, continuing to be attached to the addiction in the afterlife. Uncle Joe may be such an entity.

MRB (Mississippi River Bottom) (532 St. Philip Street)

*T*his cozy neighborhood pub is a popular rest stop on our tours. A tragic presence haunts this otherwise lively nightspot. The ghost is believed to be that of a young woman who worked in the building when it was a brothel in the 1880's. According to J.D., the owner of the bar, when the building was renovated numerous small rooms were found upstairs confirming that perhaps they were used for prostitution.

During and after the Civil War, it was not uncommon for young women to be kidnapped and then sold into prostitution. Times were harsh in New Orleans, it being one of the first cities over taken by Union. According to local legend, a young prostitute named Marie was one such unfortunate victim. She fell in love with a sailor who had been a customer. He promised Marie that he would return to marry her and take her from the life in the brothel. Although such promises were unlikely to be true, often these young women fell for them because they longed for someone to come along and rescue them from their pathetic fates. At the time, women who had been taken by many men would not have been considered suitable brides for gentlemen. For most, a life of prostitution became a life sentence. Still, Marie believed that he would return and waited for months. He never did. She would spend hours waiting on the levee, watching for his ship to return. Unfortunately, when he did return, it was in a coffin. Having died at sea, Marie was left to believe that had he lived, she would have wed. Heartbroken, she hanged herself in the courtyard. It is said she continues to wander the premises still waiting for him to return and take her away.

May Baily's
(Inside the Dauphine Orleans Hotel,
415 Dauphine Street)

*I*n the late 1890's and early 1900's, May Baily's was a famous brothel in the infamous Storyville section of New Orleans. Prostitution was legal in Storyville from 1898 until 1917, when the United States entered World War One. Today, May Baily's place is forever preserved as the bar inside the Dauphine Orleans Hotel. One sign of ghosts in the building occurs after the liquor vault is locked up at night. The bartenders have confirmed that many mornings the vault is still locked but the bottles are out and in a different position.

Reports over the years indicate that perhaps there is more than one ghost present in the bar. One is believed to be that of a Creole soldier, perhaps a patron of the brothel. Another entity, a female, seems to be very whimsical, possibly a bit disturbed. It is believed that perhaps she was employed in the brothel and eventually became an alcoholic. This would have been typical during that era. It is a common belief that the spirits of persons who were addicted during their life might remain earthbound due to the attachment to the addiction.

Yo Mama's (727 St. Peter Street)

*I*n the 1960's, this was Mr. Green's Tailor shop. One Halloween, Mr. Green decorated his shop and wanted to surprise local trick or treaters by giving them a realistic looking hanging body upstairs. A Halloween practical joke became a self-fulfilling prophecy for Mr. Green. He accidentally hung himself right here in the building. Friends and neighbors, aware of his "little joke" had no idea that he was in fact dead, until the next day when he was still hanging from the second floor ceiling!

Late at night, the bartenders report that the back door opens and closes by itself. Sometimes, a ghastly apparition with a scarred neck appears and sits at the end of the bar only to vanish a few seconds later. The owner of the bar, Art, has reported seeing out of the corner of his eye, the apparition of a man walking about upstairs. Our tour groups have in fact experienced the pranks of Mr. Green. One of his favorite ways to make his presence known is to have all of the balls in the pool table begin to hit against each other. It appears to be strictly attention-getting activity. Mr. Green is quite harmless. Photographs taken during our investigation of the bar show a mist-like substance appearing in the mirror upstairs.

The Abandoned Irish Pub (514 Toulouse Street)

*T*his building dates to 1789. In 1803, a woman named Mary Wheaton from Cumberland New Jersey married her second husband, Don Guillame Marre, the owner of the building. She inherited the property the following year when he passed away.

In October of 1806, she married a Frenchman, Joseph Baptandiere. Like many French gentlemen he engaged in the French tradition of plaçage, taking on a mistress, Angelique. By 1810, Angelique had become very demanding of him, so Joseph beat her and then murdered her by throwing her from the second story balcony. In his grief and guilt he then hanged himself in the same courtyard.

In 1818, Mary passed away on the property. All three spirits are believed to continue to reside here. For many years, the building was home to O'Flaherty's Irish Pub.

It was a lively, happy place. Live Celtic Music filled the various rooms of the pub as well as the courtyard. The staff as well as visitors experienced the spirits of those who once lived on the property. Our investigation team researched the pub in August of 1998. The owner of the pub, Danny O'Flaherty, told us that in 1987 prior to his taking possession of the building, a Voodoo ritual was in fact performed in the building in an attempt to eliminate the spirits from the site.

The courtyard was the first area where the team experienced a change in the energy. The presence of a young woman who seems to be aloof and melancholy resides in this area of the property. It is not uncommon to feel her icy touch. Most of the energy in the courtyard seems to be around the entrance to the upstairs bar and the pond. It is believed that this is the window from which she was thrown falling to her death in the well, now the fountain.

Although she probably died peacefully, Madame Baptandiere probably is emotionally attached to the property and seemed to prefer the upstairs bar overlooking the performance room. She seemed to enjoy the music on many occasions and has been seen watching the show from the balcony above. Danny O'Flaherty even sometimes sang a song for her, "Red as A Rose." Many had seen her appear when he sang her song.

The presence of Joseph was the strongest on the third floor of the building. This is where the family lived. We found a number of cold spots in segments of the rooms, in spite of the room being over 100 degrees. During the investigation we were visited by Joseph who made himself visible to us through the lens of one of the cameras. Although the actual point of focus was a dark rafter in the attic loft. The lens showed a lighted corridor and at the end, a doorway with a man standing in it. After standing there for several seconds the man shut the door quickly and abruptly. During the vision, the meter readings were high. Several of us were able to see the apparition. One of our investigators felt violent electrical impulses in her body. As soon as the door slammed, I heard a voice instruct us to leave him alone. It seems as if there was a great deal of guilt, anger and sorrow present in this spirit. The building has been vacant and boarded up since Katrina.

Ecto in courtyard of the Irish Pub

Tricou House (711 Bourbon Street)

*T*ricou House Restaurant and Bar is named after the man who built the house in 1832, Dr. Joseph Tricou. He sold the building in 1874 after the tragic death of his grandniece, Penelope. She had fallen down the staircase from the third floor balcony, breaking her neck.

Members of the staff at Tricou House have documented many visits from Penelope. One told us of countless episodes involving electrical equipment, lights, stereos and other appliances turning on and off on their own. Cold spots have been experienced sporadically throughout the courtyard and building.

We interviewed a waiter who informed us that sometimes the back doors open and close on their own and that the solid concrete statue in the fountain outside has been known to move at times. Another employee stated that the statue was originally in the middle of the fountain and has, over the years, relocated to a different area in the pond.

During a recent investigation of Tricou House, we were directed to the third floor staircase where Penelope had fallen to her tragic death. One employee informed us that she often walked down the staircase and into the adjacent disco. Our meter readings were extremely high in the disco and around the stairs although the energy "shifted around" quite a bit. One of the managers, who had spent the night in the building during a hurricane, said that she woke up hungry one morning at 3:00 a.m. She went into the office for a candy bar and began to work on the computer. She said that she could hear the pattering of what sounded like the kitchen crew downstairs. She heard the racket of deliveries being made and pots clanging in the kitchen. Deciding to wander downstairs to see who was there, she was consumed by an eerie feeling as she passed through the courtyard. The statue seemed to be facing a different direction than usual. As soon as she got to the front area, the voices stopped. As she went back towards the stairs, they began again. She walked back and forth several times and each time the voices ceased, as she grew nearer.

The management informed us that prior to 1976, the building had been an apartment house. Over the years, people who had resided there from time to time will return and inquire about the ghosts. Some of these people lived in the building decades apart from each other. In addition, the entire staff agreed that the statue moves.

The owner of the building told us the story of a man who had fallen backwards over a balcony railing, several years ago. His feet had left the balcony floor. He was caught in mid-air by something unseen and literally thrown back onto the balcony. His fall is believed to have been broken by Penelope. Penelope was believed to be in her late teens or early twenties. She is usually seen wearing a full antebellum skirt covered with ruffles. The costume that the hostesses wear to greet visitors was inspired by Penelope. As the investigation concluded and I exited through the courtyard, I could have sworn that the statue was not only in a different position but smiled as I walked by.

Turtle Bay (1119 Decatur Street)

*T*urtle Bay is a newly renovated bar and restaurant that has a number of ghostly inhabitants. Once a favorite hangout for the vampire culture of the 1990's, the establishment is now a mainstream hotspot for food, libations and lively New Orleans music.

The building is situated directly behind the Ursuline Convent, the oldest building in New Orleans. In the 1700's, this land was part of the convent's grounds, and today only a small brick wall in the courtyard separates the two properties. The Ursuline nuns originally came to New Orleans as nurses to care for victims of yellow fever and Indian attacks. The nuns also used this land, including that where Turtle Bay is now situated, to bury the dead. The courtyard is charged with energy typically found in burial grounds. In a recent investigation of this residual haunting, we felt the sensation of being pulled downward in this area.

There is an active haunting here as well. During our investigation, we discovered the presence of a female entity. Emily, once a servant here, was a petite young woman with little education. She died of yellow fever on the property and continues to reside in the upper apartments of the building and in the kitchen.

We were first called in to do this investigation when the owner of the building noticed that his clothes were soaked with water after placing them on a chair when he undressed. There was neither a leak in the ceiling nor any other explanation for the sudden water. Employees reported that kitchen appliances often turned on spontaneously. A knife flew across the room on its own and broke. The tip of the knife was never found. Recently a family on the tour captured a thick fog of ectoplasm in the seating area of the bar. The ghost seems to enjoy the music and visits from tourists, but is a bit picky as to who is in her kitchen.

Haunted Plantations

*L*ouisiana is famous for its lavish plantations that have been preserved since colonial days. Many of these historical homes are open to the public for tours and it is not uncommon to find that these plantations are still home to those who lived and died there generations ago.

Destrehan

*O*ne of the closest to New Orleans is Destrehan Plantation. It is believed to be haunted not only by the ghost of a former owner, Stephen Henderson, but also occasionally by the ghost of privateer, Jean Lafitte! Lafitte was a friend of the Hendersons and frequently visited the manor. Mr. Henderson died in 1837, just seven years after his young wife Elenore Destrehan Henderson.

Times-Picayune articles record sightings of apparitions mysteriously appearing then disappearing. Visitors touring the home have reported seeing a shadowy figure of a tall, thin man, as well as hearing disembodied footsteps that seem to roam throughout the top floor. Additionally, cold spots are found and many report feeling an occasional touch while in the home.

One woman touring the home was familiar with the rumors about the ghost of Lafitte. She called out his name into the fireplace where his ghost had allegedly been spotted. Looking up, she saw his reflection in the mirror above the fireplace. Numerous photographs of the mirror have captured the white, transparent image of a man. The staff has reported that every now and again a darkly dressed man appears outside the door and attempts to enter. When responding to allow him entry, they find that he has vanished! Another former owner is said to have made at least one visit to the manor. He had been confined to a convalescent home in New Orleans for a number of years. At a social gathering one evening, his shadowy image was seen roaming about the party only to disappear. Later, it was revealed to his wife that the man had died that night at the precise time he was seen wandering through the party!

San Francisco

$\mathcal{N}$ot far from Destrehan is the town of LaPlace where San Franscico Plantation is located. Its unique German architecture sets it apart from the usual colonial plantation. It is painted in bright, vivid blues and pastels, making it look more like a giant gingerbread house. It is beautifully decorated within as well. I brought along two psychics, Katherine Ramsland and Nora Natale, to assist in the investigation. The manager confided that she has been able to see ghosts since childhood. Although she had experienced numerous ghosts on the property, she only told us that there were three ghosts present. She wanted to see if we would pick up on the ghosts on our own, and I appreciated that.

She directed us to the large house centered on the property. As we walked toward the house, I felt a strong presence on the third floor that seemed to be the spirit of a man looking down on us. He was very protective of the property and leery of our presence. I looked back at Nora and noticed that she was aware of him as well. Energy levels were even higher on the second floor.

When we entered the second floor parlor adjacent to a small bedroom, Nora and I both felt the presence of two children. One was a very young girl, around two years of age. The other was a boy, perhaps five or six years old. A stuffed rabbit on the parlor sofa had a very strong vibration of the little girl.

After our initial exploration of the property, we returned to the office and asked about gaining access to the third floor. When we told the manager what we had experienced, she confirmed our findings, telling us the history of the family that had built the home. She said that often she is on the property very late at night and has seen and heard the little boy crying. He was the plantation owner's youngest son. He died after falling into a sugar bin, and his cry is lonely and aching. The little girl died at the age of two by falling down the stairs. She also told us that the man is believed to be Charles Marmillion, the brother of the former plantation owner, Valsin Marmillion. It is believed that Charles had suffered from genetic syphilis for a long time prior to his death. He is often seen here, usually wearing a white suit with a straw hat. When we were escorted to the attic we found the presence of Charles on the catwalk that runs along the rafters near the roof. He was a friendly presence, albeit very cautious.

The Myrtles

T he most haunted plantation in Louisiana is also the most haunted house in America! Over the years, the sounds of voices, musical instruments and a baby's cries have been heard throughout. The Myrtles Plantation, located in St. Francisville just north of Baton Rouge, was built in 1796 by David Bradford, one of George Washington's generals in the Revolutionary War. Legend has it that the home was built on sacred Indian burial ground. Never realizing the land was cursed, in 1818, Bradford left the home to his daughter, Sarah Mathilde and her husband Judge Clarke Woodruffe.

The Woodruffes had a slave woman named Chloe. One evening, Judge Woodruffe caught her eavesdropping and to punish her, he cut off one of her ears. From that time on, Chloe wore a tignon tied tightly around her head to hide the disfigurement and she secretly vowed revenge. Several months later, the family asked her to make a birthday cake for their oldest daughter's birthday. Chloe made a beautiful cake, laced with the juice of the poisonous oleander tree. Her intention was to make the family sick. But the plot backfired. The deadly ingredient killed Sarah Mathilde and both of her daughters. Angry slaves hanged Chloe that night from a nearby tree and threw her body into the river.

Chloe is one of the most seen ghosts on the property. She is seen wearing a green tignon tied around her head. During our investigation of the Myrtles, the image I captured on film in the mirror is believed to be that of Chloe. Guests and employees alike have seen the apparitions of two young blonde girls playing. In the main parlor area, visitors have often experienced feeling the children tugging at their clothes. The plantation has a wide array of ghostly photographs that they have been given through the years.

Mariah spent an evening in the Myrtles several years ago and told me of her experience. She said that during the night numerous ghosts hovered around the bed. One of them repeatedly wrapped her feet in the sheet. Each time she would remove her foot, the sheet would again be applied tightly. She later learned that the house was used as a safe haven for Confederate soldiers during the war. The servants always watched over the injured taking care to bandage them properly.

The property was purchased from Judge Woodruffe by the Sterling family. Two of their male children died while living on the property. They also had a daughter, Sara, who eventually inherited the home. She married an attorney named William Winter and had two sons and a daughter, all of whom were raised on the Myrtles Plantation.

Like many children in the 1800's, the little girl became ill with yellow fever. When doctors were unable to cure the child's illness, the Winters brought to their home a Voodoo Priestess named Cleo to heal her. Cleo's efforts proved fruitless and the young girl died. Blamed for her death, Cleo was hanged that same night from the chandelier in the ladies parlor.

In 1871, William Winter was sitting in his parlor reading to his sons, when he heard a carriage pull up outside. He then heard a man's voice yell out, "I am here to see the lawyer." When he opened the front door, he came face to face with an unknown assailant who opened fire with a shotgun. Mortally wounded, William dragged his bleeding body up the stairs of his home. He made it to the 17th step where he fell into Sara's arms and died. Many a guest has witnessed the thumping sounds of William Winter's ascent to the 17th step.

Many years later, a caretaker was murdered on the property. It has been reported that this man has been often seen by guests as they arrive. Long after his death, he continues to oversee the Myrtles.

Shortly before Halloween of 2000, I was asked by Good Morning America to do a full investigation of this plantation. I had an entire day and night to stay in America's most haunted location. Of all my investigations, I have to say that this was my most awesome experience. This time I was assisted by Midian Von Thorne and Monique Mangieri of our investigative team. We also brought along a friend of mine who had always been interested in going to an investigation, and Kristian Sonnier, who worked with the Louisiana State Office of Tourism.

We were informed that the epicenter of energy in the house seemed to be the ladies' parlor where Cleo had been hanged and that the bewitching hour of the Myrtles was 3:00 a.m. Not only did we hear music in the parlor and adjacent room, these rooms were extremely colder than any others in the house. In fact, it was so cold here that frost had actually formed on the windows. I knew at this point that the spirits were aware of our presence. They were clearly making themselves known. Non-contact thermometers confirmed extreme and erratic temperature drops.

We decided to rest in order to be able to stay awake all night. Each of us chose a room in which to stay. I had two adjoining bedrooms with a bath in one of them. As we attempted to nap, we all heard footsteps on the stairs and whispers throughout the rooms. I could hear the door to the bedroom open and close. I felt several presences standing over me, as if looking down on me as I attempted to sleep. I suddenly felt heaviness, on my legs. It felt as if a very small child was sitting on my legs. All the while, I never felt uneasy or afraid of them. I felt very peaceful and protected. I fell into a very deep sleep.

I awoke to the scent of gardenias in my room. It was reported that this was a sign that Sara Winter was present. It is said that she would walk through the home during her life and spray floral perfume throughout the bedrooms. Some of the others on the team reported smelling cigar smoke in their rooms.

Later that evening, we walked the property videotaping in night shot. We captured numerous orbs not only outside but also throughout the inside of the house. In one outdoor shot, we captured what looked like the legs of a man walking through the trees. The following week, one of our tour guides, returned to the Myrtles with friends. He filmed a large orb that floated around for about twenty minutes between the main house and the gift shop near an outdoor lamp. It appeared in the exact location where an apparition of Chloe had been captured on film.

Chloe

Placing audio recorders throughout the house that evening, we were able to capture voices in practically every room of the house. One recording revealed not only voices and footsteps, but also the sound of a woman screaming at the end of that segment.

Around 2 a.m., the temperature in the main parlors rapidly returned to normal and the frost left the windows. We began to communicate with some of the spirits. The first was a little girl, but she was quickly replaced by an older female spirit we believe to have been Chloe. She gave us very little information, and it seemed as if the spirits were more interested in being acknowledged than giving data. We decided to simply enjoy the magical ambiance in the room and not risk making these spirits feel uncomfortable. For the next hour we simply spoke to them and experienced their presence. At exactly 3 a.m., we felt them leave. We were all left with very happy, peaceful feelings. The Myrtles is not just the most haunted place in North America, it is the most enchanted.

Oak Alley

*A*nother plantation housing friendly, comforting ghosts is Oak Alley. One is believed to be that of a former owner who watches protectively over the property as visitors sense the aroma of his cigar smoke. Occasionally, a door slams by itself to announce his presence. In addition, a little girl has been seen walking about the house from time to time. Believed to be the daughter of the first owner, she died here at the age of twelve.

Perhaps the strangest sighting that tour guides and guests at Oak Alley have reported is that of a lit candle flying across a room of the mansion all by itself.

Popp Fountain

Popp Fountain, The Time Warp in City Park

Several years ago, I was approached out of the blue by an old friend. She had found out I was writing about the supernatural in New Orleans and asked me if I had ever investigated the Time Warp in City Park, near Popp Fountain. I have lived in the city all of my life but I assured her I had heard of no such thing.

She shared with me an experience a mutual friend had thirty years ago. Grant Cooper and some friends, all teenagers at the time, had been in City Park one afternoon. He had described to her finding himself in a tree with another young man and neither of them remembering how they got there. She went on to say that years later, in her late twenties, she began to date a man who had recently moved here from New York. He described to her exactly the same incident happening to him, only many years after the incident with Grant. She told me that over the years she has from time to time come across people who have all experienced the same thing.

I asked Grant Cooper to give me an account of his experience and this is his story:

"New Orleans is known for its many strange and supernatural stories, replete with Voodoo queens, vampires and more. Mixed in with these stories is a tale of the time warp in City Park. City Park has a long and celebrated history over the past 100 years which includes its famous Dueling Oaks, the huge moss-strewn live oak trees which, for previous generations, served as a site where men dueled to the death to protect their honor or exact revenge.

"I first learned about the time warp from direct experience as a teenager of 18 in 1970. I had spent a long, lazy day with my friends exploring the park and enjoying its beauty. At one point, we even swam in one of the shallow lagoons, climbed trees and generally had a great time. Although my memory from nearly thirty years ago is patchy, I distinctly recall that all of us experienced time dislocation. We were near Popp Fountain and for whatever reason, we all felt that we had lost track of not only the time, but even what day it was.

"At this point, it would be helpful to note that no drugs or alcohol were involved. I'm sure you're thinking, 'Okay, so everybody loses track of time every so often, and everyone can even lose track of whether it's Wednesday or Thursday or whatever.' But we *all* lost track at once and had a very strange feeling that we were in a different time. And we knew *nothing* about this phenomenon and its connection to City Park. In fact, it was only much later, in recounting our experiences to others, that we were to learn that the time warp in City Park is truly a part of the history of this city which has been experienced, shared and recounted by many New Orleanians."

In fall 2000, I began teaching a paranormal course at the University of New Orleans. The class included field trips to haunted locations for investigations. Because several of my students had experienced strange time changes at Popp Fountain, we chose it for one of our investigations. Everyone noted a definite change in energy upon entering the fenced off area around the fountain. Meter readings were high and irregular, temperature changes were noted and several participants found orbs on their photographs. The most obvious activity was the smell of burned sugar. The entire area that we know today as City Park had once been a sugar cane plantation. The odor we experienced was a residual of the sugar cane fields that would be burned down after the harvest to make them ready to replant for the following year.

The Mysterious Swamp

*T*he Manchac swamp, just west of New Orleans on the shores of Lakes Pontchartrain and Maurepas, has always been known for the strange things that occur there after nightfall. Even the Indians believed it was cursed, long before Europeans settled in the area. Pirates supposedly hid their treasure there. It is believed that every time a pirate hid treasure in the swamp, another pirate would be killed at that location so his spirit could guard the treasure. A pirate's treasure is said to be cursed forever, along with his soul. Those fortune hunters who disturb the treasure awaken these restless spirits. A "fifolet" (French for false fire) is an eerie burning ball of blue misty light. It is believed to indicate a treasure buried nearby. Follow the fifolet and you will be led to hidden riches. We found many newspaper articles documenting fifolet sightings across the state.

When the railroad was being built along Lake Pontchartrain on the outskirts of this bayou, most of the workers camped out in the woods along the inlet. Late one evening, a couple of those workers were awakened by a strange blue glowing light. Peering out of their tents, they saw that ball of light move into the woods. The men dressed quickly, grabbed a shovel and followed it. They had heard about the fifolet from local people but, not believing in the curse, they continued to follow it further and further into the woods. It suddenly stopped and disappeared, as if it had been sucked up by the ground.

The men began digging up the earth where the ball had vanished. After furiously burrowing about three feet they suddenly hit a solid chest. This had to be a pirate's treasure. The thought of gold can provoke strange and powerful emotions in men. One of the two grabbed the shovel and struck the other over the head, rendering him unconscious. He then picked up the chest and attempted to carry it away. To his dismay, he found he could not lift either of his feet. It was as though something in the ground was pulling him into the soft, swampy earth. He began to scream and struggle, but the more he tried to break free, the deeper he sank. His partner began to regain consciousness, only to see his workmate neck deep in what appeared to be quicksand. He watched in horror as the man and the chest sunk into the ground. Running back to his tent, he lay awake, afraid to sleep. Had the pirate's curse followed *him* back to camp?

The next morning, he made his way back through the woods to the spot where the blue ball had led them. The shovel lay on the ground. The ground was solid. There was absolutely no evidence that any hole had been dug or that any quicksand had ever existed. As he walked away with the shovel in his hand, he could swear that he heard laughter in the wind. He quit that day, never to return. There are tales of a moss-covered pirogue, a Cajun flat bottom boat, ferrying the doomed souls of those who ventured through this swamp in search of treasure.

Ghosts of pirates are not the only entities haunting the Manchac Swamp. In the early 1800's, a slave trader sold a group of laborers from Africa to a wealthy man in New Orleans. The man's other slaves immediately recognized this group as being from a deadly tribe of African headhunters. After being told about these cannibals, the man went back to the slave trader and furiously demanded he take them back, which he did. But instead of sending them back to Africa, he took them up river to Baton Rouge, where he sold them to a plantation owner. These cannibals murdered their new owner, his family and the other slaves on the plantation. They then disappeared into the Manchac Swamp and word of the carnage spread from Baton Rouge to New Orleans.

The British Army was sent into the swamp to capture these dangerous headhunters. Their orders were to kill them all and place each head on a wooden stake in the swamp. Eventually all were found and killed, their skulls remaining in an eerie and fearsome display for a long time afterward. Many people in this area fear that the ghosts of the cannibals remain, preying not on the flesh of men but upon their souls.

Prior to 1915, this area had been the farming town of Frenier. It was one of four towns in this area originally settled by Germans. In 1850, its population was only 900, among them an old woman of color named Julia Brown. She used to amuse herself by sitting on her porch playing her guitar and singing songs that she made up. Her favorite songs contained self-made lyrics about taking half of the town with her when she died. "When I die, I'll take half Frenier with me," she would sing. Folks were never sure if Julia was a Voodoun, but after her death on September 28, 1915, many people were convinced that she was.

On the day of her death, she was laid out in her casket and people came from as far away as New Orleans to pay their respects. If nothing else, Julia Brown was well liked. Her funeral was supposed to take place the following day. As her casket was being lowered into the ground, dark clouds hovered over the town and the wind began to howl. Within seconds, raging hurricane winds of over 100 miles per hour were flinging casket and mourners alike in all directions. Within minutes, Lake Pontchartrain swelled and a 25-foot wave devoured the tiny town. There were fewer than 100 survivors. Julia Brown floated out of her coffin and was found several days later in the swamp, along with many other bodies. There were so many corpses that all had to be buried in a common grave as they were, with no coffins. They all were buried on what was once an Indian shell mound. Today, nothing remains other than thick brush, home to poisonous snakes. But late at night, you can still hear the howling wind and distant screams of anguished souls. In the background, you can even make out the voice of an old woman singing. To this day, many people believe Julia Brown was a Voodoun and actually predicted that disastrous storm of 1915.

Another legend from the swamp is one brought to New Orleans by our French forefathers. They also brought over another misunderstood creature of folklore, the werewolf! Legends of witches turning men into werewolves or becoming werewolves themselves can be found throughout history, particularly in France. The French called this beast the "loup garou." Here in Louisiana the Cajun slang was "rougarou."

Once the soul of a man is cursed to be the loup garou, he will become the dreaded creature, roaming the nearby swamps and devouring whatever or whoever crosses his path. Cajun folklore even says that the werewolves even gather for loup garou Balls. It is said that they fly in on bats and dance together under the full moon.

Those who become the loup garou by choice, casting spells to shape shift, can reverse the spell themselves. Legend tells us that if you survive an attack of the loup garou, then you *too* will become one. Should you go out in search of the creature and *your* eyes meet *his* red glowing eyes, then you too, will become the loup garou. Like the legendary vampire, the loup garou can bite and drink the blood of its victim as well as devour his flesh. Once the curse is passed on, the previous victim is freed from the spell. If the creature becomes injured or killed, they will instantly become human again. If you do meet eyes or survive an attack of a loup garou, telling no one of the incident for a year and a day, you may be freed from the spell as well as free the spirit of the attacker. There is no known protection from the attack of the loup garou.

Countless tales have been told throughout the generations all over Louisiana about those receiving the curse of the loup garou, or even worse, being born with it. There are people who live in the French Quarter today who will swear to have seen one. Like the vampire culture, there are people who even claim to be werewolves. Symptoms of werewolves are similar to that of the vampire's victim. Those who bear the curse experience heightened senses, cravings for raw meat, animal-like dreams and unexplained blackouts, particularly around a full moon. Accounts of strange dog or wolf-like animals have existed since colonists settled the area.

Several years ago, I experienced something near one of the swamps just outside of New Orleans that cannot be explained rationally. I was driving down the interstate highway about 2:00 a.m. It was a very foggy night, I could barely see beyond my headlights. Traveling at about 70 mph, I raced past something standing in the middle of the road. It stood on two legs and was covered with gray matted fur. As I sped past it, it did not move a muscle. It just stood there. I looked in the rearview mirror but could see nothing in the fog and the blackness. I was far too frightened to go back and investigate. I do know that whatever it was, it appeared to be taller than my van. I saw only the legs. I heard no sounds. However, as I passed the creature, I experienced one of the foulest odors I have ever encountered. To this day, I do not know what it was. However, I *do* know that it certainly was not fearful of a speeding van and it was like nothing that I had ever seen before.

The most recent account of an alleged loup garou sighting was told to me by the owner of a local swamp tour company. His nephew, who lives along one of the bayous on the outskirts of New Orleans, had been trapping out in the woods surrounding the swamp. It was getting close to sunset, so he began to make his way back to his boat. Suddenly, he came upon a gray creature about the size of a large dog. In fact, he believed it was perhaps a wild dog. He claimed that within several seconds the animal began to growl and snarl, a swirling gray mass of fog surrounded it as it appeared to grow even larger. According to this bizarre account, the animal stood on two feet, howling and wailing. The young trapper fell to the ground crawling out to the shore of the bayou and into his boat. He maintains that he never looked back as he sped away. Being so terrified by the experience, and believing in Cajun legend, he never spoke a word of the incident until a year and a day had passed.

One legend from the late 1890's tells of a wealthy gentleman from New Orleans who moved to the bayou and took a young woman named Madeline to be his bride. He had often heard stories of the rougarou from her family. One evening while he was visiting a local pub, he heard a young hunter and trapper bragging about his kills. In a drunken state, he challenged the young man to go out into the swamp and kill the rougarou, offering him a large sum of money for his catch.

The next day the young hunter left on his journey. When he returned late that evening, he told a story of being attacked by a large wolf-like creature. He fired his gun at the beast scaring it away, but not before taking his knife and cutting off the creature's left paw. He held out the bloody bag for the gentleman to see. He quickly opened up the bag and pulled out not a wolf's paw but a slender hand of a young woman. The hunter stared in disbelief. The gentleman recognized the ring and hurried home to find his beloved Madeline with a shawl wrapped around her left arm. He demanded that she remove the shawl. When she did, he saw that there was nothing more than a mutilated stump at the end of her arm! Because she was injured, the spell had been broken.

Two years later, Madeline gave birth to a baby boy. The child was born with a small crescent shaped birthmark on his back. The midwife saw the mark and said, "He is bewitched!" The child had been born with the mark of the devil. "He'll be fine, as long as you keep your eyes on him when there is a full moon." Shortly after the boy was born, the couple hired a young woman named Michelle to help care for him. She was a rather strange girl, with funny shaped eyes, who always wore a cloak hiding her face. But she had shown up just as they need a nanny for the child and she seemed very mild natured.

When Michelle saw the birthmark on the child's back she told her mistress, "It is the mark of the rougarou. He will be one by his 16th birthday." The young mother became frantic. She had thought that the evil curse that once gripped her had been lifted and now it seems as though she had passed it on to her little baby. She asked if there was anything she and her husband could do to save the child. Michele told her to kill a white pigeon and smear its blood on the birthmark. Then they were to place the child on a soft blanket under a full moon. She said that the moon would draw up the mark and the curse would be lifted. The next full moon they carried the child into the woods, armed with a shotgun, to wait for the full moon. As the moon rose a large wolf-like creature with red glowing eyes appeared. It stood snarling over the child. The parents ran toward the wolf screaming and firing the gun grazing the beast on the left side of its neck in an effort to scare it off, but it was too late. As it howled off into the woods, its jaws dripped with the blood of the infant child. Later, they found Michelle lying in the woods. Her neck had been blown open by a shotgun and she had bled to death. The spell had been broken. But the legend says he who breaks the spell and tells the tale before a year and a day has passed will become the rougarou. No doubt Madeline and her husband told no one, but what became of the young hunter that freed Madeline?

Another strange creature said to reside in the swamps of Louisiana is a mermaid-like creature. Many Native tribes told stories of a mermaid goddess who sings a haunting melody. In the early 1960's, a fisherman saw a beautiful girl floating in the bayou. Thinking that she needed help, he made his way toward her. When she saw him coming, she dove beneath the water. As she arched her back out of the water he saw that the lower portion of her body had the scales and fins of a fish.

Bayou Manchac

NEW ORLEANS
VOODOO

Ritual artifact masks

Kifwebe

Sacred Objects

On some of our tours, we loan participants spirit shakers imported from Africa, Haiti, South America and Mexico, used in actual tribal ceremonies to call on the spirits of protection.

In Voodoo, the belief system is based on a primary supreme deity and several demi-gods called "lwa." It has been compared often to Catholicism which believes in one God yet has many saints. Another focal point of Voodoo is ancestor worship. In Voodoo ceremonies, spirit shakers are used to call upon the ancestors and the lwa. Ceremonial items, masks, knives, carvings, can often be purchased in New Orleans at Voodoo shops, such as Reverend Zombie's where we start our Voodoo and Haunted tours. Tourists are often concerned about potential spiritual attachments of these articles. Quite often, the items are merely replicas of the authentic items and have not been actually used in ceremonies. However, occasionally, pieces can be bought that are originals. And sometimes they *are* still quite charged with life force, or ashé.

We interviewed Mr. Andy Antippas, owner of Barrister's Gallery located at 526 Royal Street in the French Quarter, for better understanding of this phenomenon.

"With the exception of a few decorative pieces, all the tribal artifacts we sell at Barrister's Gallery are real. By that, I mean they were used in rituals. They are charged with energy through sacramental use. Theoretically, the energy in the artifact remains dormant with the piece because it has been removed from its sanctuary and sacred chants, oils and offerings are required to activate the protective spirit within the wood carving. I say *protective* because all tribal carvings, for the most part, are concerned with commemorating mystic ancestors, or with protections of the clan, family or individual for whom the piece has been carved."

Mr. Antippas told us that in his twenty years of operating Barristers Gallery, he has sold thousands of artifacts to collectors. "During all these years, I've heard many stories from collectors who give me the impression that certain acquired objects hanging on a wall or sitting on a table are like batteries which, from time to time, their 'terminals' are capable of spontaneously discharging their protective powers. I've often been told of masks constantly swiveling on their hook until they were placed elsewhere on the wall. Also, of standing figures which reorient themselves by turning to look in different directions. One woman swore to me that a Balinese mask she bought from us moved across the room on its own."

He shared one very interesting story in great detail. He told of a mask called "Kifwebe," which translates into "the mask."

"Two neighboring tribes in Zaire, the Basonge and the Baluba use them. They are two basic forms: Round (Baluba) and vertical (Basonge). The mask at issue is Basonge. The shape of the Basonge mask emulates the head of a certain kind of lizard. It displays bulging eyes, a large crest (male) or a small crest (female), and long, protruding, pursed lips." He explained that both tribes held this type of mask to be the most curative mask in all of Africa.

"One of my collectors told me that late one night, their infant developed a raging fever which they could not quell and their pediatrician was nowhere to be found. She told me that she and her husband were frantically trying everything Dr. Spock recommended, to no avail. She confided in me that she remembered my telling her that the lips on the female Kifwebe mask that they had purchased from me some months before were pursed because they were shown sucking the fever out of the sick. She retrieved the mask from the library, caressed it, implored it for help, and placed it under the child's crib without her husband noticing. Within minutes, the fever completely disappeared. With great hesitation, she told her husband what she had done, and pointed to the mask under the crib. He responded by lifting up the mask and kissing its lips. To this day, they remain convinced that the mask may have saved their child's life."

Voodoo Hysteria

*I*n 1791, a slave uprising in Saint Domingue, today Santo Domingo, brought to New Orleans free people of color and their Voodoo religion. These people had no knowledge of European history and had certainly never heard of the Inquisition. They had no reason to believe they could not come to this city and worship freely. The first Voodoo Queen in New Orleans was Sanité DeDe, a young woman who had bought her way to freedom. She held rituals in her courtyard on Dumaine Street, just blocks away from the Cathedral. The rhythmic beat of the drums could be heard during mass!

For this reason, the Church decided in 1817 that no religion other than Catholicism would be allowed to be practiced within the city limits. It was in Congo Square, now Armstrong Park, where the early Voodouns held their rituals. Here, Voodoo began to evolve into its own New Orleans brand. It was intermingled with other slave tribal religions and also with Native American customs. The Natives sympathized with the Voodoo practitioners as they had with the Islenos, and taught them about the plant life in the area. Eventually much Spanish and French culture was blended in as well. Even today, New Orleans Voodoo is very different from the purer form found in Haiti and Africa.

The roots of Voodoo have been traced all the way back to Africa. Dating back thousands of years, it is one of the world's oldest religions. In his book, "A Brief History of Voodoo: Slavery & the Survival of The African Gods," Andy Antippas gives an overview of its fascinating history. The Yoruba people of Southwestern and Eastern Dahomey and Togo/Nigeria founded a great city called Ife. It is from the religious beliefs of Ife that Voodoo as we know it today has evolved. The home of Voodoo in Africa is what is now known as Benin. It is estimated that by the 1750's, 30,000 slaves a year were brought to Haiti and, with them, the Voodoo religion. In the language of the Dahomey tribes, the word "Voodoo" means gods or spirits. The Dahomians believed that these spirits had the ability to enter the worshippers. This was believed to be a valuable experience, warding off illness and misfortune.

The Voodoo religion is based on one main supreme deity, God, the creator, and thousands of spiritual "helpers" called "lwa." The lwa are much to Voodoo as the saints are to Catholicism, each one serving a specific purpose. Each lwa has a specific symbol, called a "verver." These symbols are usually traced on the ground with corn meal to summon the lwa during rituals.

Ancestors and spirits of the dead are also revered in Voodoo. Altars are made to honor both lwa and ancestors. Food, beverage, tobacco and favorite items are placed on the altars to honor the spirits.

The two aspects of Voodoo are the Rada and the Petro. Rada lwa are cooler and slower acting. Rada is the religious and healing side of Voodoo. Petro deals more with spell work. The petro lwa are darker and hotter, although faster acting. Another important sect of lwa are the Ghede, the dead. They are the closest to humans therefore are fast acting. It requires a bit more fortitude in dealing with them, however.

The most important lwa in the Voodoo pantheon is Papa Legba. He is the guardian of the crossroads. Without him, you cannot communicate with the other lwa or with the ancestors. His verver is represented by the cross. In other religions, he is known as Ishu, Elegua, or Elegba. In the Catholic saint pantheon, he is closely associated with St. Peter. He is the great trickster of the lwa and is usually seen as an elderly man with a cane. His colors are red and black. Legba enjoys cigars, rum, sweets, especially coconut, chicken, and anything shiny or gaudy. His altar is usually placed near a doorway as he is the gatekeeper, guarding the veil between men and gods. He is the remover of obstacles. He is associated with the sun and daylight. His female counterpart, associated with the moon, is Erzulie Freda.

Mistress Erzulie is the lwa of passion, pleasure and prosperity. Candles are lit in her honor on Thursdays and Saturdays. She is the most beloved in the pantheon as well as the most beautiful and sensual. She is the lwa of dreams and hopes. She deals with issues of the heart and relationships and she loves the finest in all things: champagne, flowers and jewelry. It is her representation of unconditional love that associates her in the Christian pantheon to Mother Mary. Her symbol is the heart and her colors are blue and pink. Her sister, Erzulie Dantor, represents revenge and jealousy. Her symbol is a heart with a knife plunged into it. Her favorite cuisine is a black pig and peppered rum. Dantor is the protector of women, especially single mothers.

One of the most supreme and powerful lwa is Damballah-Wedo, the serpent god. He is represented in Voodoo rituals by a snake. The dance with the snake symbolizes the unity between our world and the world beyond, as the dancer and the snake become one. Damballah is the great healer of the pantheon. He is the closest to God's consciousness, his color is white.

Offerings to Damballah are usually cornmeal and eggs. His wife, Aida-Wedo, is represented by the rainbow.

The great warrior of the pantheon is Ogoun. The Ogouns are the protectors as well as the healers. Their colors are red and black. Offerings to Ogoun would include rum, cigars, metal, knives, swords, and athames. His Christian equivalent would be St. Michael.

Baron Semedi is the head of the Ghede. His day is Saturday. He is represented by a skeleton wearing a top hat and smoking a cigar. The Ghede rule the world of the dead and are protectors of children. Because they are so close to our world and the world of spirits, they are also great healers. Their worldly connection makes money one of their favorite offerings. They also enjoy rum, cigars, and Pall Mall cigarettes. His female counterpart is Mama Bridgette. In Haitian folklore, Baron Samedi fell in love with the Celtic goddess, Brighid, and brought her back to rule the underworld with him. LaSiren, or Yemaya as she is called in Santerian traditions, is the great mother of the sea. She is also the protector of women, especially mothers and their children.

In spite of Voodoo's benevolent nature, many New Orleanians feared it. Tales of Voodoo curses swarmed through the city and this mystical, spiritualistic religion now spawned fear and hysteria in New Orleans, shrouding the Crescent City in a veil of superstition that spilled over into our folklore for over one hundred years. Voodoo hysteria lasted in New Orleans well into the 1950's and left behind a trail of folklore and legend of Voodoo queens and root doctors who have become ingrained in the City's history.

In February 1932, the *Times Picayune* printed an article about these rituals of "wild and uncontrolled orgies" and "serpent worship." Police actually arrested participants and frequently broke up rituals! In 1863, the *Times Picayune* recorded the trial of one such arrest. Approximately 400 women had been arrested and were tried for the crime of "dancing naked at a Voodoo ritual."

It seems a young woman accidentally walking into the area had reported the crime to the police. After a three-day trial, the women were released for lack of evidence when the girl who reported the "crime" became strangely confused and was unable to testify properly against them. Many believed that the Voodouns hexed the girl and then charmed the judge. Because of such incidents, many a ritual was relocated in secret to the swampland on

Bayou St. John, near what is now City Park.

In 1944, Robert Tallant wrote a book on Voodoo portraying a dark and sinister picture of the religion. As a white journalist of that era, no doubt, Mr. Tallant was somewhat biased in his portrayal. However, there are newspaper articles and police reports that do substantiate some of the activity that gave way to the hysteria. There were some practitioners who did prey on the fear and superstitions of the white Catholics. It was not uncommon then for crosses of death, tiny coffins, and strange concoctions or voodoo dolls to be found at dawn on the doorsteps and galleries of residents. Sometimes there would be just a black candle or a black crepe wreath. Superstitious residents of the times would constantly seek protection from such curses. Many of the Voodoo practitioners' spells that were sought after were for protection or uncrossing, removing hexes. One of the most common practices to protect one from evil curses was to scrub the front stoop of the house with brick dust. Many New Orleanians purchased gris-gris bags (good luck charms), and wore them near the body or placed them in the home.

In a 1924 newspaper article, doctors at Charity hospital told of patients being brought in wearing their gris-gris bags and refusing to part with them. Doctors attested that in many incidences, victims would fear that they would die if the bags were taken from them. There is documentation that in some instances, once the bag was removed, a victim's heart would stop. Many of the incidents considered Voodoo crimes that we found in the police reports were actually crimes committed not so much because there *was* a curse but merely the *belief* that there was.

In a New Orleans *Daily Picayune* story dated August 13, 1863, simply called "A Snake Story," a young woman by the name of Susan Williams claims to have snakes inhabiting her belly. She alleges that she had become the victim of a Voodoo curse. She had gone to several practitioners obtaining roots and herbs to rid her of the dreaded serpent. The results of her endeavors were quite shocking. Rather than expel a snake from her belly she gave birth to a baby. She attributed the pregnancy to witchcraft and "expressed her opinion that a child brought unto the breathing world would never come to good." In the morning the baby was dead. Ms. Williams died the following day in Charity hospital.

In 1938, Reverend Howard Randle believed his wife, Lucinda, had put a spell on him. She had always been a very jealous woman. He had been having an affair with a young woman on Rampart Street and had also been seen frequenting several of the local bordellos by numerous individuals. Night after night, his poor wife, tormented by his liaisons, cried and prayed that his escapades would cease. But instead, the situation worsened. He had been spending less and less time at home and more time with his mistress.

In an attempt to win his fidelity back, Lucinda visited Dr. Rockford Lewis, a local witch doctor who operated on Royal Street. She bought a powder to turn her husband impotent. She carefully emptied the small bag into his coffee one morning. When he began to drink it, she became afraid that it might kill him so she cried to him that she had poisoned him. Within a few moments, she had convinced Howard that he was going to die!

Overwhelmed with guilt, she fell to her knees, begging him to kill her, so that she wouldn't be left alone. Believing that he would soon die, he walked with her out to the levee. She laid her head on his lap and gazed out onto the dark river. She talked of how she would go first and be waiting for him by the river in the glorious afterlife. They would be together forever! Slowly, he took the knife out of his coat pocket and she closed her eyes. He plunged the blade into her throat, ripping it open. He, of course, did not die, but he probably wished he had. He spent the rest of his life in prison. Legend says Lucinda still wanders the rivers edge, waiting for him to join her.

Voodoo can also seek revenge as well. In 1932, Elijah Wheatley dragged his girlfriend, Lucille Williams, to a canal where he threw her in and she drowned. A night watchman saw Wheatley running away and he reported the crime to the police. The newspaper printed the story the next day. The family, of course, wanted justice. As they prepared Lucille's body for her funeral, they placed a fresh egg in each of her hands. A rope was tied around her wrists and she was laid face down in the coffin.

For the following two days, they kept a vigil over the body. Tall red candles burned at each end of her coffin. She was then buried and the eggs crushed and sprinkled around her grave. The morning after her funeral, Elijah's body was found floating in the same canal, in the same spot where he had killed Lucille. Police assumed that maybe he had become remorseful and perhaps committed suicide. The family had a different opinion.

On November 2, 1950, neighbors called the police to an apartment at 808 Dauphine. The neighbors complained that they heard the screams of children within. When the police arrived, they found Rosita Zerruda in a frenzied state attempting to burn down this building by dousing it with kerosene. She was arrested before she could ignite it. The woman had deep gashes in her arms that were obviously self-inflicted. A thick trail of fresh blood led police to a bedroom where her four children lay in pools of congealed blood, gashes down their forearms. The family was rushed to Charity hospital. The children were treated for their injuries and eventually released into the custody of a relative. Once treated for her wounds, Rosita Zerruda was admitted into the psychiatric ward.

When questioned by police, Mrs. Zerruda hysterically explained that her neighbor, a Voodoun, had cursed her. She informed police that when she awoke that morning, she found blood smeared on her doorstep, along with a black wreath. Police never got any more information out of Mrs. Zerruda. During her questioning, she began to stutter, and her pupils dilated. She mumbled senselessly as her skin grew pale and clammy. Her body twitched as her pulse weakened. Mrs. Zerruda slipped into a coma before their very eyes. Never awakening, she died in Charity Hospital within several months.

In October of 1951, in a quiet neighborhood near the New Orleans lakefront, a woman shot and wounded her husband for burning salt and incense on their front door. Convinced her husband was trying to put a hex on her, she was driven by fear and superstition to attempt murder. Police rescued her before she could pull the trigger on herself. She, too, was committed to the Charity Hospital's psychiatric ward.

The Mysterious Tomb of Marie Laveau

Author with TV crew at Marie Laveau's tomb

$\mathcal{N}$ew Orleans' most noted Queen of Voodoo was Marie Laveau. She was born in 1783, to Marguerite Darcantel, a slave from Haiti and mistress of a wealthy plantation owner, a Frenchman, Charles Laveau. I mentioned in an earlier chapter about plaçage during the colonial days of New Orleans. In this arrangement, children of the union had right of heirship, and bore the father's name. The children would also be reared in the father's religion, Catholicism. Marie was raised on her father's plantation. She was educated and studied to be a hairdresser. She was a devout Catholic, who went to mass every day of her life. She was a dark skinned woman with long black hair that she frequently wore in a single braid making her look much like an Indian or a Gypsy, probably adding to her mystique. In 1819, she married Jacques Paris, a native of Saint Domingue, in the St. Louis Cathedral. Upon her marriage, her father gave her property in the French Quarter. A short time later, her husband was killed and she was to be referred to as the "Widow Paris." Since there is no documentation of his death, it is suspected that he possibly left her. Rather than risk losing respect in the community, she insisted that she was a widow.

She later became mistress to Christophe Glapion with whom she had numerous children. Some accounts speak of her having as many as 15 children, but it is believed that she actually only had three daughters, one of whom was also named Marie. Most people believe that she rose to the heights that she did, due to her ability of being inside the homes of the aristocrats and having the opportunity to know their personal business. It was believed that she had spies amongst the servants in these homes that helped gave her insight to what was going on in their lives.

As a hairdresser, she also worked nursing those in need. Back then, hairdressers and barbers could do minor surgical procedures such as removing warts and moles. She could help with sore throats and minor stomach distresses as well. She would take in the sick and nurse them in her home, regardless of their race or ability to pay. She also would minister to prisoners on death row alongside Père Antoine.

She became interested in herbal healing and studied herbs under Sanité DeDe. No doubt Voodoo had been her mother's religion, and she became very interested in it as well. In spite of her attraction to Voodoo, however, she never abandoned her Catholic roots. She had an intense awareness of the similarities between the two, particularly between the Voodoo lwa and the Catholic saints. She incorporated the use of candles and Holy Water in Voodoo rituals. It was because of this blending of religions that the white Creole Catholics began to find Voodoo a bit more palatable. Marie retired as Queen in 1875. Although throughout her reign many a New Orleanian feared her, when she died at the age of 98 in 1881, others believed she was a saint. Her life was surrounded by rumors and gossip set off by fear and hysteria. It has only been in recent years that the public is realizing what a great humanitarian she was

Our company offers daily tours of St. Louis Cemetery #1, where Marie Laveau rests today. Thousands flock to her tomb to make wishes and leave offerings of thanks. Her tomb is covered with X's, believed by some to be a Voodoo ritual to ask for blessings from Marie Laveau. This activity in fact has nothing to do with Voodoo, and very few of these X's are circled to indicate that the wish has been granted. Yet each day, grateful believers leave offerings of thanks for favors bestowed. Everything from flowers and Mardi Gras beads, to food or even money can be found at the site. Remains of candles that have burned down give evidence of rituals at the tomb. Several of our tour guides have received significant assistance from Marie Laveau simply by putting a hand on her tomb, sincerely asking her for help and leaving a meaningful offering. We encourage this respectful manner of making a wish and can vouch for its effectiveness.

Many a story has come from the experience of visiting Marie's tomb. One couple from Tennessee sent us some original negatives that had been taken during one of our tours. The woman wrote that during the tour she had walked up to the tomb and made a wish. She claimed that while she had her hand on the tomb praying, she heard the voice of a woman speaking to her. She believed this to be the voice of the ghost of Marie Laveau. The woman left an offering in thanks to the Voodoo Queen, took some photographs and joined the rest of the tour. When the couple got back home, they had their film processed. Much to their surprise, the photos all came out except for those taken at the tomb. They sent us the negatives for observation. All of the pictures taken before and after the site of the tomb are fine. The five that were taken around the tomb are completely blank, as if unexposed.

Throughout the generations, locals and visitors driving past the cemetery late at night report seeing the vision of woman in white walking through the darkened city of the dead. Some legends say that ghostly Voodoo rituals are still held near Marie's tomb, as she appears draped in a large serpent overseeing it.

An employee of the Louisiana State Museum told us an interesting story about a portrait of Marie. She said that when the Museum was being repaired, a portrait of Marie was brought to another branch for display. When the museum staff opened the wrapper around the portrait the back of the painting was covered with scratch marks "as if something from within tried to claw its way out." There was no rational explanation whatsoever for the strange scratches on the back of the painting.

Apparition appearing over tomb of Marie Laveau

Marie Laveau's Legacy

*M*arie Laveau's daughter, also named Marie, went on to become Voodoo Queen when her mother retired. Marie II was much more enterprising than her mother. She commercialized Voodoo. She opened up a shop on Bourbon Street where she sold herbal remedies, roots, and spells. She was best known for her love spells and wealthy people paid well for her work.

Sometimes things did not work out the way they had expected. There was once an aging, wealthy bachelor, who had fallen hopelessly and foolishly in love with the daughter of a business associate. He asked for her hand in marriage and his associate, who was having financial problems, readily agreed. The girl was young enough to be his granddaughter and swore that she would rather die than marry him! Not only that, she had given her heart to a young adventurer who was exploring the West Indies in search of his fortune. She had promised to wait for him.

The father wanted to be wealthy more than he wanted his daughter to be happy. He and his friend visited Marie II for help in arranging a wedding. Marie listened intently to their woes and agreed that the wedding would take place. She gave the girl's father some powder to place in her food every night for the next week. She also gave the older gentleman some herbs that she said would help with his impotence.

After a week had passed, the girl, pale and sick, went to her father and told him that she had changed her mind. She agreed to marry the old man. Two weeks later, the wedding was held in the Cathedral with a reception in the nearby Grand Ballroom. As the old man danced his young bride around the ballroom for his guests, he began to gasp for air. He swayed back and forth as his face turned red, then blue. He collapsed to the floor, dead of a heart attack. The father was horrified and blamed himself for using Voodoo. He went to Marie II and accused her of trickery. Marie smiled and said, "There was no trick, a wedding is what you asked for and a wedding is what you got." The story of course had a happy ending. The father got exactly what he had asked for and the young woman became a very wealthy widow who eventually married the man of her choice.

By today's standards, Marie II would have been considered an enterprising businesswoman. Her siblings however, felt it was wrong for her to have used their mother's name and religion to profit. When she died, they denied her burial in the Glapion family tomb. She was buried in an unmarked grave in St. Louis Cemetery # 2, along with slaves.

Marie Laveau's House of Voodoo, located at 739 Bourbon Street, still operates, selling spells, gris gris, and other Voodoo items. There are two altars in the store, one to Marie I and the other to Marie II. The store proprietors tell us that if a visitor leaves an offering for Marie I, someone must match the offering on the altar of Marie II, otherwise she gets jealous and things will literally fly around the store.

During the filming of our video, "Journey Into Darkness, The Trilogy," our videocameras captured ectoplasm over the face of the actress portraying Marie Laveau at Marie Laveau's House of Voodoo, 739 Bourbon Street

NEW ORLEANS
VAMPIRES

History of Vampires in New Orleans

*V*ampires and vampire-like creatures have been found in the folklore of every civilization, every culture and every religion since the beginning of recorded time. New Orleans is no exception. Vampire hunts began in the early 1200's in Eastern Europe, and over hundreds of years this practice spread into Western civilizations. By the time New Orleans was settled in the early 1700's, this practice was rampant in Europe. Vampire hunters, usually church representatives, were digging up the dearly departed, driving wooden stakes through the corpses, then beheading and burning the bodies.

Causes of vampirism vary. One could be predisposed at birth by being been born at certain times of the year (new moon, holy days), or being born with a red caul, with teeth, or with an extra nipple. If a child was born with excess hair, white hair, red hair, a red birthmark, or with two hearts, the theory persisted. The seventh son of a seventh son was believed to be doomed to vampirism. Vampirism was suspected upon the death of a child if he or she was weaned too early, suckled after weaning, or died without having been baptized. If a pregnant woman received a curse or was stared at or attacked by a vampire, the child would be cursed to vampirism. This type of predisposition was considered a genetic defect, like a mutation, and vampirism was considered inevitable.

The onset of vampirism could occur after birth as well. Typically, being fed upon seven or more times without dying would guarantee one would become a vampire. Practicing sorcery or witchcraft, eating sheep killed by a wolf, leading an immoral life (prostitutes, murderers, alcoholics, rapists) were causes as well. Suicide, death by violence or by drowning, or dying without the benefit of Last Rites could lead to vampirism. Even after death, it was believed vampirism could be induced by no burial or improper burial rites, or even a cat jumping or a shadow falling over the corpse and/or coffin.

Fortunately, there are ways to prevent vampirism should any of the above occur. Placing coins or dirt on the eyes, tying the mouth closed or stuffing it with garlic were common practices to prevent a body from ever returning from the grave. Our ancestors would cover mirrors and stop the clocks in the home of the deceased. In Louisiana, many families still practice a custom called sitting up with the dead. When a family member dies, someone within the family or perhaps a close family friend stays with the body until it is placed into one of our aboveground tombs or buried. The body is never left unattended. The most common reason given for this practice today is respect for the dead. This tradition however, dates back to vampire folklore in Eastern Europe where they were watching for signs of paranormal activity. If a cat was ever jumping over, walking across or standing on top of the coffin, if a dog was heard barking or growling at it, or if a horse shied from it, these were signs of impending vampirism and at that point steps would be taken to prevent the corpse from returning from the dead.

Common practices included burying the corpse face down and burying at a crossroads. Family members often would place a sickle around the neck, tie body parts together or mutilate the body, usually by decapitation and placing the head at the bottom of the feet. The most prevalent remedy for impending vampirism was to drive a stake into the corpse, decapitate it and then burn the body to ashes. This method was the only way to truly destroy the undead.

By the 1700's, these practices were rampant throughout Western Europe, particularly in France and Germany, where many people were emigrating to New Orleans. Believers insist that vampires could have been smuggled over in ships with the settlers. The early French settlers brought over brides from Europe who transferred their belongings in large wooden casket-like boxes. According to folklore, even though vampires prefer the night, they are not destroyed by daylight. Although they generally hunted and fed at night, it was common for vampires to walk about during the day. There would have been no need to smuggle them in coffins in the hulls of ships. This idea was popularized by fiction writers such as Bram Stoker. More likely, vampires would have boarded the ships like anyone else and blended in well with society.

The first written text on the treatment of vampirism, "De Graecorum hodie Quirundam Opinationabus," was published in Greece by Leo Allatius in 1645. Twelve years later, a French Jesuit priest named Father Francois Richard wrote a text linking vampirism to witchcraft. He based this on opinions he had formed after reading the "Malleous Maleficarum (The Hammer of Witches)," written by two Dominican priests during the Inquisition.

In 1746, Dom Augustin Calmet, a French biblical scholar, published a study of vampires in Eastern Europe entitled "Relation de ce qui s'est passé a Sant-Erini Isle de l'Archipel." He became the most noted vampirologist of the 18th century. The reanimating of corpses was believed to have been the work of the devil himself, leading the Roman Catholic Church to declare that vampirism was not only evil but also satanic. It was at this time that holy water and crucifixes were believed to ward off or destroy vampires. Concurrently, the Eastern Orthodox sect made similar decisions regarding vampires and the church. The idea was then adopted that a vampire was either a witch who had died or the child of a witch. According to French folklore, there existed a magical vampire creature called the Melusine, part woman and part serpent, who would fly through the air wailing.

In 1345, the first documented vampire hunt took place in France. Frenzied villagers reported attacks shortly after the death of woman believed to a witch. They exhumed her body, drove a stake through her heart and burned her body to ashes. The church continued to hunt vampires until the beginning of the 20th century.

About 95 years later, another real vampire arose in France. Gilles de Rais was a general who fought with Joan of Arc and was considered a hero in his country. Ultimately, however, he was exposed as a black magician and a murderer, a sexual deviant who derived pleasure from torturing young boys to death in sadistic rituals and then drinking their blood. After he was convicted and sentenced to death in 1440, his body was strangled then burned to ashes.

If being a murderer, rapist, or other criminal element predisposes one to vampirism, it is easy to see how vampires could become prevalent in New Orleans. The city's original citizens were criminals and likely all of them would have been predisposed! Once they blended in with the mortals, they could easily feed on the population without raising much suspicion. After all, with people dying here in such great numbers, who would really notice another body here or there?

New Orleans has always had a high murder rate, not to mention a lot of missing persons. The French Quarter has always been a very mysterious and seductive place. Runaways commonly come to the French Quarter to hide out, as do people with pasts. Many have inexplicably disappeared, some of whom were never known to have been here in the first place. If no one knows you are here, how will they know if you should disappear? If you just drifted in, people will assume you just drifted out.

For generations, folklore has told of vampires hiding out in colonial caskets in the attic of the old Ursuline Convent. Many have told tales of shutters, long since sealed, suddenly appearing open in the middle of the night, only to be shut again in the morning light. Others believe that early priests captured the vampires and locked them away in the attic. Tales are told of thousands of blessed screws holding down the shutters to keep the vampires in and the daylight out. Since vampires can shape shift into a mist, it is foolish to believe that sealed shutters would contain them!

One very cold January evening several years ago, I ventured down Chartres Street shortly after midnight. As I walked past the convent, I suddenly felt as if I were being watched by many eyes. The sensation I became aware of can only be described as evil. For the first time on any property, I suddenly became fearful. I felt a cold chill down my spine. I left the block quickly and not since have I returned there alone so late. Several years later, while investigating another property, I ran across an old paranormal report on the convent. It quoted a caretaker stating that he felt as if he was being watched from the third floor. He described the same chill in his spine as I had experienced years before.

What can be the explanation for the shutters being open and then closed? What can explain why hundreds of people have reported a face sometimes seen in the tiny window of the convent? Or the eerie feeling of a thousand eyes peering out in the middle of the night on that block? Possibly these are merely superstitions, manufactured in the human mind and spawned by fear. Or maybe there is some truth behind the legends.

Vampirism and Disease

*V*ampires were often blamed for disease. In Europe, plagues and tuberculosis alike were often blamed on vampirism. Tuberculosis patients often coughed up blood, leading doctors in the Middle Ages to believe that they had been ingesting blood. Thus came the belief that the disease was caused by a vampire bite. The word "nosferatu" literally means plague-carrier. Early cemeteries in Louisiana were often situated far from towns, many times at a crossroads, to discourage the spirits from finding their way home. Often these tactics were called "confusing the spirit."

In many cultures, vampirism is believed to be nothing more than aberrant behavior resulting from adverse mental or physical conditions. Porphyria, a human blood disorder, is believed by many to be a condition that has resulted in many "diagnosed" vampires. The patient suffering from porphyria becomes extremely sensitive to light. Skin lesions may develop and the teeth become brown or reddish-brown in color. The gums recede giving the canine teeth a fang-like look. Like the diabetic who replaces insulin with injections, blood transfusions can be effective in reversing the effects of porphyria. It is believed that in medieval Eastern Europe, nobleman may have been instructed by their physicians to drink blood to reverse the disorder. Because so many royals had a tendency to marry within the same family, it is easy to see how recessive genetic disorders such as porphyria may have been more widespread among the ruling classes.

Vampirism is not always caused by genetic defects or acquired through predisposed conditions. One of the most common ways to become a vampire is to be fed upon by a vampire numerous times. But the feeding habits of the undead are systematic. Classically, if a vampire is to return from the grave to feed, the first visit it will make is home. It will feed on the immediate family first, the blood the closest to its own being the sweetest. Eventually, it will make its way into the village, but rarely will it go after a spouse. The spouse usually is not the same bloodline and besides the vampire had other uses for its spouse. The vampire was known for its ravenous sexual appetite and it would continue to have relations with the spouse.

There are legends throughout folklore of those born half mortal and half vampire. Known as the "dhampir," these offspring would inherit the supernatural abilities of the immortal parent. While the dhampir usually would not feed on the living, they nevertheless had the ability to see through the guises of the undead and therefore could easily destroy them. Since vampires would be attempting to blend in with the living, it would require superhuman senses to be able to detect the subtle differences. Many dhampir hired themselves out as vampire killers because of these hereditary abilities, and children of the dhampir would inherit these talents as well.

Vampire Lifestyles

Throughout the 1990's, New Orleans was home to a subculture of people who considered themselves to be vampires, living in what we called "vampire reality." Many of these so-called vampires were merely imitators. They had become entranced with what they had seen on the movie screen, enticed by the thought of immortality and eternal youth. Some are actual blood drinkers because in movies and in novels, vampires traditionally drink the blood of their victims. More times than not, the vampire is a male and the victim female.

In reality, vampires come in both genders and not all of them drink blood. These vampires are not the immortal type on the movie screen, but mortals. They look like anyone else and even have ordinary jobs during the day. But these vampires have a secret side of their life when they engage in blood drinking. The modern mortal blood drinker is not necessarily what you might visualize.

Only a very small minority of these people resort to violence or murder to acquire their food. Most are very discreet and go about their activities in legal and humane ways. Some have donors, some exchange sex for blood and some belong to blood cults and exchange only within their own clans. Are they blood fetishists or vampires? Is there a difference? Many believe there is not.

The psychic vampire takes psychic energy, or life force, from its victims. It is not so much the blood that is of interest to this vampire but the life force within the blood. Drinking blood can be messy and rather inconvenient. Mortal vampires also risk disease such as AIDS and hepatitis. Taking psychic energy is a feat anyone can perfect. In the early stages of this type of vampirism, it is common for the vampire to have to touch the victim in order to take his or her energy. As the predator becomes more adept, usually through meditation and ceremonial magic practices, touch is not necessary to accomplish the transfer. It is at this level that the vampire can transfer the energy through the eyes. The eyes have often been called the windows of the soul. The victim may not even be aware of what is happening. Vampires throughout history have had this ability to mesmerize through the eyes.

The transfer of thoughts or mind reading is also achievable. This is probably where Bram Stoker got the idea to give his character that famous hypnotic stare. Many of these vampires can learn to drain energy from across a room. Have you ever known anyone that made you tired just being around them? In the Middle Ages, if one's spouse was boring and put people to sleep, they were believed to be a vampire and treated as such upon their death. Once the vampire has mastered his skills, he becomes able to astral project over his victims and prey upon them in their sleep. According to Konstantinos, in his book, "Vampires: The Occult Truth," the intentional psychic vampire is probably the most dangerous type of all vampires. He estimates that one in every five individuals will suffer this type of an attack!

Not all psychic vampires are intentional, however. Often, chronically ill people can be psychic vampires and not even realize it. We are all familiar with the typical scenario of an elderly couple in which one is very ill. How often has the sick one lingered for years and the healthy one who has served as caretaker suddenly dies?

Some researchers believe that when mortal psychic vampires die, many will remain earthbound in spirit form and continue to feed upon the living. Until recently, this was attributed to witchcraft. Some even once called this type of attack a "hag attack." Here in New Orleans, the French called it a "cauchemar," or nightmare witch. Commonly referred to as a "mara," from which the word nightmare is derived, it is a phantom or ghost-like creature that feeds on the living, usually just before they fall asleep. The victim can usually sense a presence in the room; some report seeing a shadow of the predator during the actual attack. Once the victim is literally pinned down by the creature, there is heaviness on the chest. Most are rendered temporarily paralyzed and unable to scream. They are conscious of what is going on around them, yet unable to move or speak. When the creature has finished feeding, the pressure is released and the victim then falls into an unnaturally deep sleep. Many times, the attack is remembered as a dream. Very often in folklore, the victim remembers the attacker only as standing over him gazing down. There are even cases where vampires have actually entered a victim's dreams or have taken one on an out of body experience. Usually, a good night's rest will rebuild the energy supply and no residual harm is done. However, if the attacks continue and the victim is fed upon enough times, he or she may also become a psychic vampire!

Another type of psychic vampire, the sexual vampire, can be either mortal or immortal. The mortal sexual vampire takes energy through sexual contact. The immortal type attack as do the mara, but the attack is sexual in nature. A male immortal sexual vampire is called an incubus and the female a succubus. They often leave marks on their victims, rendering evidence of the attack. One woman claimed that what made her different from a sex addict was that she needed the energy she derived through sexual contact as opposed to just being obsessed with sex. She did admit, however, that her condition had a negative impact on her life and that she rarely had long-term relationships because of this.

It is estimated that possibly one in five individuals suffer a psychic vampire attack in their life. Repetitive psychic attacks can cause extensive damage to the energetic system leaving the victim weak and immune deficient. One then becomes pale and weakened, more prone to sickness and accidents, even depression and suicide.

You can protect yourself from psychic attacks by being grounded at all times. Avoid being in altered states such as those induced by drug use, and be careful with hypnosis and meditations. Do not engage in magic with people you are not familiar with. White light meditations are helpful, as are aura cleansing, such as sage smudges. Information on these things may be found in most occult bookstores.

I received an unsolicited e-mail from a woman who had recently visited New Orleans. She said that her husband was a Baron from Iceland, a descendent of Danish Kings. He had spent several years in England and was described by her as an adept High Priest in Kabbala Magic and a metaphysician. She went on to describe a Count that he had become acquainted with in England who had relocated to New Orleans. She described the Count as a physician and a vampire. He supposedly saved her husband's life from another vampire who had intended to feed on him. This Count was said to now have a shop in the French Quarter. Her husband supposedly had the ability to be able to recognize vampires by their smell and their aura. He even taught her how to spot them. She went on to describe incidents where she and her husband located several vampires and vampire hunters in the French Quarter during their recent visit.

A young man from London took our Vampire Tour and shared with us a fascinating story involving an encounter that he had in his hometown. I became especially interested in talking to him when he expressed his familiarity with the history of Jacques St. Germaine, who had spent several years in England. This young man claimed to have been fed upon by a blood drinker on numerous occasions. The final feeding was to the point of near unconsciousness, and then the blood drinker cut himself and bled into the young man's mouth. He swallowed the blood. He said he had a scar to prove that the feeding had occurred, below his left shoulder blade, right over the aorta! He backed the idea that real vampires blend in to society. He did not dress differently or behave like vampires portrayed in movies. He was rather quiet and not at all obvious.

One woman was a vampire role player. Although admitting that it was "only a game," she still dressed in vampire attire right down to having fangs made for her teeth. Becoming obsessed with living her life like a vampire, she slept late and only came out at night and even then, only with sunglasses on. She made a point of drinking only the reddest of wines, eventually graduating to real blood -- not human blood, however. She purchased blood of cows and pigs from slaughterhouses! She also dined on rare meat, claiming it satisfied her urges.

One young man from New York was the classic imitator. He know little about vampires, vampire folklore or history. He knew the essentials though, saying that he had to wear sunglasses because the sun "really did hurt" his eyes. He stayed awake at night and slept days. He made mock blood drinks of orange juice and tomato juice which, mixed together and left at room temperature, coagulate. Otherwise, he drank dark red wine. I asked him what attracted him to the vampire lifestyle. It turns out his mother had died just a few months before and his grandmother shortly before that. He did not know his father. Rather than deal with the sadness of death, this young man seemed to embrace a lifestyle that promised life forever, claiming that he decided to become a vampire so he would not die. He never claimed to have been attacked or fed upon. I truly believe he was not familiar with that part of the legend.

Another young man I interviewed several years ago on one of our tours swore that his family lineage was from Romania and that he was a direct descendent of the real Dracula, Vlad the Impaler! He insisted that his canines, filed to a point, were natural. He also confided in me that he even kept a box of home dirt in his apartment, thus proving his vampire heritage. I was convinced that he certainly knew a lot about the fictional character, Dracula, but he had not even done enough research to realize that the real life Dracula was not a vampire at all. I found his claim of being a vampire himself unconvincing.

Some lifestylers consider their condition a disease. This theory seemed to apply to some of the blood drinkers and psychic vampires alike. They truly believe that they have a medical condition that requires them to obtain energy from others. Most of these blood drinkers will admit that it is not so much the blood as it is the life force within. The average amount of blood taken during a feeding is only about a teaspoon. Most responsible blood drinkers are well aware that they are not immune to blood borne pathogens and select donors carefully. Most of the lifestylers I interviewed had no delusions of immortality. They believed that their disability was similar to diabetes, but they need blood instead of insulin. They believe that if they do not feed, they will become sick and weak.

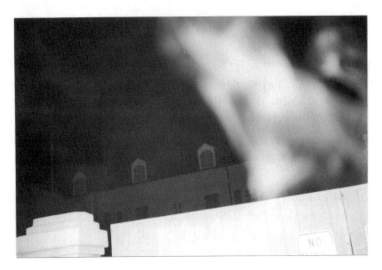

Strange fog over Ursulines Convent

The Magnetic Doctor (714 St. Peter Street)

*M*urder has plagued New Orleans since it was settled in the 1700's by French prisoners and other undesirables. Crimes involving vampirism have been prevalent throughout our history. Etienne Deschamps, known to most as the Magnetic Doctor, was also a magician, dabbling in hypnosis and mesmerism, and a psychic and medium of sorts. At the age of 75, Deschamps became infatuated with a twelve-year-old girl named Juliette Dietz.

He befriended her family and over time enticed the young girl into trusting him to perform experiments using his mesmerizing abilities. On January 20, 1880, he lured her into his St. Peter Street home, sending away her younger sister who had arrived with her. Once he lured her inside, he chloroformed her and, according to the newspaper account, "debauched her in a fiendish manner." The younger sister, feeling uneasy, went home and told her father that something was wrong. By the time the police arrived and broke down the door, it was too late.

Juliette's nude body lay dead on the bed. The Magnetic Doctor, also nude and realizing he had killed her, began to slash himself repeatedly with a knife. He was arrested, tried, convicted and executed for the crime.

The hypnotic activities of Etienne Deschamps fit the profile of psychic vampirism. Classically, mesmerism and high ceremonial magic are common practice with those who are vampiric. Many believe that the old magician's goal in his experiments were to steal some of the girl's youth and vitality through sexual contact, thus making him a sexual psychic vampire. The newspaper account of his trial even stated that he never intended to kill her. Her death was deemed accidental, the result of administering too much chloroform. He was grief stricken over having killed her and that is why he was also attempting to kill himself.

According to Deschamps' testimony, she had insisted that he use chloroform, showing that there was some willingness on her part. Also, his testimony indicated that she was afraid of experiencing pain during the experiments, again suggesting that perhaps it was sexual. In spite of this, there was no evidence of rape found at her autopsy. This is another clue that leads us to believe that it was her vitality and life force that interested him.

In his book, "Liquid Dreams of Vampires," Martin V. Riccardo notes that records of hypnotism or mesmerizing being associated with vampirism are evident as early as 1589 in Italy, from a written work called "De Fascino." In 1653, a Spanish physician, John Lazarus Gutierrez detailed the symptoms of mesmerism in his work, "Opusculum de Fascino." The symptoms are identical to that of the vampire's victim. The notion of vampires possessing the ability to hypnotize and steal the life force is found in every civilization's history and folklore. According to Mr. Maritn, a report written in 1949 in Eastern Slovakia describes the vampire having the ability to destroy with a "single glance." Hypnosis, seduction and mastery are all common characteristics of vampires.

The Legend of Jacques St. Germaine
(1041 Royal Street)

*I*n 1903, a young man from the South of France, named Jacques St. Germaine, claiming to be a descendent of the Compte St. Germaine, an 18th century alchemist, migrated to New Orleans. He occupied a house on the corner of Royal and Ursulines Streets for a very short while, and then disappeared mysteriously, after attacking and biting a young woman in his French Quarter home. After escaping and reporting the crime to police, she later died in Charity Hospital. After the authorities walked through his home to find he had abandoned it, they confiscated from his personal effects a collection of wine bottles filled with wine *and* human blood! In addition, bloodstains were found throughout the home. They were of different sizes and different ages. It is undetermined how many people may have been brought to his lair, not having the opportunity to escape. There are people who believe that this man was the Count himself. Many people believe that he is still alive today, possibly still *in* the city.

There are certain cults that even worship St. Germaine, believing that he was an Ascended Master. Such groups have been found all over the United States and as far away as South America. Certain individuals have claimed to have known him. Still others claim an ability to communicate with him to this day.

The house that was occupied by Jacques remains vacant to this day. We started investigating this story in 1996. The current owners are nowhere to be found, yet all expenses on the property are paid to date. What is even more mysterious than owners who do not wish to rent, sell or occupy such a grand house is the fact that no one has ever vandalized it. One tiny exterior lock keeps vagrants and vandals out. The energy surrounding the house borders on indescribable.

Several years after the Jacques St. Germaine incident, a string of violent murders hit the city and again had vampiric undertones. The twentieth century vampire began to break away from traditional biting of the victims. The new generation of blood drinkers began using more sophisticated methods of draining their victims.

Colin and Damon Wilsons's book, "Killers Among Us," documents that in 1918, a number of residents in the French Quarter were murdered by some mysterious visitor in the night. The murders remain a mystery even today, as no one was ever arrested. No credible evidence was ever found. We do know that the murderer used an ax upon victims. There were even eyewitness reports from several people who managed to escape the grips of the phantom ax murderer. One description was of a "shadowy figure" hovering over a bloody body. Another witness walked into her home to find a family member dead and to see a mysterious shadow of a man "disappear as if he had wings." The silhouette of an ax-wielding intruder was all that anyone ever reported. The murders ceased in 1919 and began again for a brief period and again ceased. Gaping neck slashes, shadowy figures and vanishing figures all caused whispers of vampires again in the streets of New Orleans.

It was during my investigation of the Royal Street house that had once been the home of Jacques St. Germaine that I personally experienced an attack. It was not a physical being I encountered, but a phantom creature, a mara.

Prior to the attack, I experienced a series of strange vampiric dreams. (Often throughout history, vampire attacks are remembered by the victim as a dream.) During these dreams, I saw everything red as if looking through the eyes of some sort of animal. Most of the dreams involved the feeling of flying or leaving my body. I was accompanied by an unseen male vampire. He transported me to the French Quarter. I flew above with my own guide who showed me the lairs of the true vampires. In one dream, I was attacked and bitten by a small wolf-like creature in Pirates Alley. I would awaken from each dream, shaken and completely drained of energy. I became all the more interested in my pursuit of information on Jacques. One evening, as I walked down Ursulines Street, I was stopped by a man who was inquiring about a neighboring guesthouse. We spoke for about twenty minutes, standing outside of the mysterious house.

Later that night, while lying in bed, I felt the presence of someone entering my room. Being involved in so many investigations, I often had visitors follow me home only to find their way back to the Quarter. I could sense that the energy was different, this was no ordinary ghost! I ignored the presence until it hovered over top of me. Then without warning, its heaviness fell upon me. I looked up to see nothing there. But I could feel the weight bearing down on my chest. I could not scream or move. After several minutes, the heaviness ceased and I fell into a deep state of sleep. I woke with a feeling of numbness in my left shoulder blade.

I continued to lead tours and investigate the story. For the following several months, each time I would stand in front of the house and tell the story, I would again feel the tingling sensation in my back. I often would lose my voice while telling the story, only to regain it after I would leave the location. One evening, as I strolled through the quarter with a friend we came upon the corner where the house sat. As we neared the corner, she doubled over in pain. The closer we came to the house, the more her anguish increased. As she described the sensations in her abdomen, I could feel them in my own body. She remained ill for some time after the incident, vowing never to return near the cursed house.

On another occasion, as I walked past the house, I suddenly flashed a mental picture of what was attacking me from the property. I saw, in my mind's eye, a tall, gaunt man, with wolf-like eyes that glowed red. His hands were long and thin with long claws. He was pale and drawn. I saw this image for only a few seconds. Two months later, a woman from Texas, who was taking the tour, described exactly the same vision at the location. Then the attacks ended as abruptly as they began.

A young man who works in a local restaurant approached me and told me of a strange encounter he had with someone that he believed to be a vampire. In August 1998, the French Quarter experienced several nights of an electrical black out. Underground systems failed and transformers blew up. During one of the longest periods of darkness, the young man found himself walking down Chartres Street at about 11:00 p.m. Darkness blanketed the Quarter.

As he crossed at the corner of St. Peter and Chartres, he noticed another young man dressed in black leather standing in the dark against an unlit lamppost. He immediately found this to be odd, considering there was a heat index of over 100 degrees that night. The young stranger asked him for a light for his cigarette. As he lit the match for him and held it up to his cigarette, rather than thanking him, the man replied, "It's a nice night out for Jack." Not knowing how to respond, he turned and continued his walk down Chartres Street. After turning at the corner of Chartres and Toulouse Streets, he said that he heard a swoosh sound behind him. He found that "Jack" had abruptly come up behind him with what he described as abnormal speed.

He stated, "It was like he landed there... He didn't walk up, I felt like he landed behind me. He was right next to my head, staring me dead in the eyes. His eyes were almost a fluorescent shade of blue, practically glowing in the dark. Within seconds he was gone. He walked abruptly past, uttering not a word, disappearing into the darkness." The man is convinced that the mysterious stranger was a vampire and for some unknown reason decided not to attack.

What intrigued us most about this encounter was the line about "Jack." We may never know what he was referring to but we do know that Jack in French would be pronounced "Jacques." These legends in our City's history are sometimes impossible to confirm or validate. Yet, mysterious murders and disappearances continue to occur here in massive proportions.

I interviewed a woman who claimed to have had a similar experience with someone we believe to be the same man. She was walking down Bourbon Street one evening when she noticed a "beautiful man" out of the corner of her eye. She said his mouth did not move but she heard him speak. She said he called her by her name and then vanished into a carriageway entrance. "I ran over to see who this curious being was, but when I arrived I saw that the entrance way was chained and locked. It was as if he disappeared into thin air."

Several days later she experienced another incident. "I was again walking down the street. Lost in thought, I was looking down at the ground, not paying attention to what was in front of me. Then I suddenly saw a pair of boots. I looked up and there was the same man. He had dark hair and pale gray eyes. His skin color appeared to be someone of Mediterranean descent. He asked me for a light. I told him I did not smoke. He replied, 'That's too bad, because it's a nice day for Jack.' He then held out his hand."

She said that his hand was thin, with long, sinewy fingers and claw-like nails. "When I took his hand into mine I felt nothing. Sure, I felt his flesh, but no energy, no life. Suddenly I heard someone walk up behind me. I dropped his hand and turned to see a couple walk up. As I turned back around, he had vanished. Approaching the couple, I asked, 'Did you see me talking to that man?' The woman said yes, but when we looked he was no where to be seen."

That night as she lay in bed she heard something outside her window. Looking at the window she saw the same man. His hands clung to her window screen.

What is odd about this scene is that her window is on the second floor. There is no balcony outside. She screamed alerting her husband and daughter. When the others came to the room, she watched in horror as the strange man on the screen, moved quickly in a horizontal sweep from the window. Upon examining the window the next day, several tears were in the screen in the direction that he moved. Tear marks that looked as if they had been made by an animal's claws.

A little closer to home, a young man that we had considered hiring to do tours for our company, experienced a strange metamorphosis after experimenting with vampire cult activity. When the young man first approached us, he was attractive, lively, and very theatrical. He had all the qualities that were necessary to be a tour guide for the company.

But shortly after he began to study for the position, something strange began to take place with him. He had become very intent on learning as much as he could about the vampire lifestyle. He began hanging out in noted vampire bars. At first we were amused at his sudden ability to mesmerize, particularly young ladies. After all, he was young, in his twenties, and his antics seemed cute. But he became obsessed with vampirism. He eventually became involved in activities with blood cults, diminishing his time in training. We saw less and less of him.

Something had taken hold of him. Rumors that he was a blood drinker began to stir among the streets of the French Quarter. His lack of appetite had begun to show. He became thin and gaunt. With each passing day he grew pale and lethargic.

The last time anyone saw him; it was as if he had gone completely mad. His skin was so cold and pale; he looked as if he really were dead. He kept talking about Jacques St. Germaine, his favorite story on the tour. He spoke of Jacques as if he knew him. He mentioned something about "Jacques" leaving New Orleans and having asked him to go along. No one, of course, took him seriously, until he disappeared later that same day. He has never been seen or heard from again. This was only within days of the blackout incidence.

The Legend of St. Germaine

The Brothers

In May of 1932, a little girl staggered into the French Quarter police station and reported a heinous crime. She said a stranger had enticed her off the street and led her into an apartment. Once there, she was tied to a chair by two brothers who cut her left wrist and drained some of her blood into a cup. They then drank her blood, bandaged the wound and repeated the act for the next three nights. Luckily, she managed to escape one day while the brothers were out. When officers converged on the apartment, the brothers had not yet returned, but the apartment was hardly unoccupied.

In another room they discovered four more victims. An adult male, an adult female, a fourteen-year-old boy and a dead nine-year-old girl were found tied to chairs, their left wrists bandaged. In yet another room, the police discovered seventeen dead bodies stacked on top of one another, all completely drained of blood. The brothers were eventually captured, tried and convicted. They were executed in 1936 in a very crude electric chair. A doctor examined them and, finding no heartbeat, pronounced them dead. They were buried in one of our aboveground cemeteries.

Since then, prowlers have been reported in the building more than 22 times. Official police reports contain descriptions of these intruders which exactly match the appearance of the brothers just before their execution. They are not ghost-like, but solid. Are they ghosts or are they vampires? When their tombs were opened one year and one day after their burial, the coffins were found to be completely empty. No trace whatsoever of bone fragments or even dust was found.

And what of the survivors? Vampire legend tells us that if one is fed upon by the undead seven or more times and survives, he becomes a vampire himself. Of the four survivors, only the little girl who reported the crime suffered no long-term effects. She had been fed upon only four times, and there is no indication that she ever went on to drink the blood of others.

Although the adult female survivor had been fed upon seven times, there are no records that she ever went on to drink the blood of others. However, upon her release from the hospital, she was transported to a mental facility where she spent the remainder of her life.

The adult male survivor, also fed upon seven times, began keeping a diary in which he described increasingly bizarre dreams involving blood. After many months of these nightmares, he went on to murder 33 people over the next several years, drink their blood, and dissolve the bodies in acid. He disappeared in 1949, around the time a similar killer in England was executed for his crimes. The diary was found many years later in a cottage on Bourbon Street undergoing renovation.

The 14-year-old boy had been fed upon the longest, eleven days! There are no records that he ever went on to drink the blood others. Sadly, however, he was murdered by his own father, burned to ashes in the family home. The father was later committed to a mental institution for life.

Contemporary Killers

*N*ot all vampire murders happened a long time ago. Rumors persist from the early 1970's of a young man who killed and butchered his best friend. Not only did he drink his friend's blood, he froze the fragmented body so he could feed upon its flesh at a later date. As the legend goes, he was institutionalized for life. His trial was supposedly covered up at the request of his rather wealthy family. Was this only a rumor? Perhaps it was, but vampire crimes continue and some do make the headlines.

In the late 1970's, the bodies of two females were allegedly found on the steps of the chapel adjacent to the Ursuline convent. The bodies were said to display three and one half inch lacerations behind the left shoulder blades and were drained of blood. Some believed these murders to be the work of some cult or gang, but an arrest was never made. Still, there are those who are convinced this was the work of vampires.

On the night of November 25, 1996, in a small town in Florida, four teens led by 17-year-old Rod Ferrel entered a small cemetery. Believing themselves to be vampires, they held a ritual involving animal sacrifices, sex and blood drinking. They were welcoming a new 15-year-old girl into their cult. After this ceremony, the group went to the girl's home where the leader beat her father with a crowbar until his face resembled ground beef. They also brutally beat her mother to death in the kitchen. After drinking the blood of the parents, the "vampire teens" got into a car and headed for New Orleans, finding their way to the French Quarter. They spent several days here and were then captured attempting to flee to Baton Rouge where Ferrel's mother lived at the time.

A local business owner was found dead in his apartment in 1998. Even more hideous than the Florida vampire murder, this victim's head was beaten off completely and it was determined that he had been decapitated with a blunt object. The murderer was never caught.

In the summer of 2003, a businessman attending a convention in New Orleans spent an evening at the Dungeon. There, he became intrigued by a group of people who claimed to be vampires and invited them to his hotel room. In the morning, hotel staff found him dead in the hot tub. His skin had been removed! One type of vampire that is seldom heard of is one who is referred to in the Charleston area as the "Boohag." The legend of this creature stems from the Gullah people who settled off the coast of South Carolina. The Boohag is a vampire who takes not the blood but the breath of its victims. Not having a skin of its own, the creature steals the victim's skin and wears it as his own until it is worn out. The creature uses the skin to appear human to unsuspecting victims then replaces it with new skin. Similar vampire creatures can be found in Norse folklore as well. Were the killers of this man duplicating the actions of the dreaded Boohag in their murder, or was something more supernatural at play here?

Such murders continue to plague the city of New Orleans. Many locals believe that deaths due to vampirism still occur regularly here and that such murders are covered up. With all the homeless in New Orleans, certainly the public does not hear about each individual who turns up dead or missing. In fact, most disappearances probably go unnoticed.

Revenge of The Succubi

*B*oth the incubus and the succubus are known as vampire-like demons. The incubus (male) was thought to slip into a woman's bedroom and force her to have sex. The succubus (female) was thought to engage in similar activity with males. These are psychic vampires who drink a person's energy rather than his or her blood. They are highly seductive and irresistible to mortals. If fed on for too long by one of these vampires, one may soon find a need to sustain oneself by feeding off of the psychic energy of others through sexual contact.

The large building on the corner of Chartres and Governor Nicholls Streets was once a community sports center where neighborhood teens could gather for sports and social events. In the early 1950's, a handsome, young coach was hired. He had a boyish smile, a gentle voice and a charm that could easily seduce the hearts of innocent teenage girls. In no time, he became notorious for taking advantage of young girls at the center.

By 1954, he was having his way on a regular basis with three high school seniors who had known him for a couple of years. Each believed *she* was his only one. None of them knew about the others until one afternoon when one of the girls accidentally happened upon his diary. He had recorded details of many sexual liaisons, including the full names of the two other girls who attended the center. They decided to band together and confront him, threatening to go public with his journal. That was the last anyone saw of these girls.

What became of them remains a mystery. Three weeks later, the coach was discovered dead in his apartment, lying nude on the bed. His lifeless body was sticky with congealed sweat and bodily fluids. A coroner's report indicated that he had sexually exerted himself.

Parapsychologists believe that the girls were violently murdered by him and that they returned as succubae, for revenge. The journal disappeared and resurfaced in the 1960's as an underground publication, only to disappear again. But the story continues to survive as part of our vampire folklore.

Séance for a Vampire

*W*hen I first met with Katherine Ramsland during the Gothic Convergence in New Orleans, she informed me that her next book would be on ghost hunting. We kept in contact and when she returned to New Orleans, I invited her to stay at our home. I was very familiar with her work, particularly her most recent, "Piercing the Darkness: Undercover in America with Vampires." I had recently read the book and was fascinated with her experiences. Her book ended with a living vampire, Christian, committing suicide in an attempt to become a stronger vampire. If his spirit remained earthbound he was now immortal, meaning he had become a mara! Katherine wanted to learn to hunt ghosts so that she might find this creature.

She possessed a ring that she was convinced once belonged to this person. She also believed that his spirit was attached to the ring! We began our hunt by taking the ring to several psychics and asking them to tune into the ring's energy. Some were right on, others missed it. All those who tuned into it agreed that there was something evil associated with it. Those most sensitive to its energy immediately dropped the ring, some even bursting into tears. We knew we needed to do more than this to communicate with this spirit. We decided to conduct a séance!

The night before the séance, we attempted to contact the ghost using the psychic board and pendulum. We asked several questions to identify the ghost as the one associated with the ring. Usually when I work with the pendulum and board, they agree. This time they did not. At first, it appeared that the ghost was responding to us favorably then he changed. It was as if he mocked us in our attempt to identify him. I grew very tired in the attempt. Several times I almost fell asleep. About 1:30 a.m., I convinced Katherine that we should give up and try again the next day.

I lay awake in bed that night, unable to sleep in spite of the fact that I was exhausted. Something kept enticing me back to the board, so I slowly made my way back up to the third floor and then collapsed on the futon. I stared over at the board, too tired to move. Yet every time I would close my eyes, it was as if the board called out to me, taunting me to try once more to unravel the mystery of the ring. My physical body won the battle and I drifted deep into sleep. The following day, I was engulfed in a state of depression that can only be described as emotions that were not my own. It was a peculiar yet familiar experience. There was a heaviness from him that surrounded me.

Mariah joined us the next day and we briefed her on what we had experienced the night before. Mariah reluctantly took the ring and immediately sensed that a spirit was attached to it. She told Katherine that the ghosts of the victims were following her around! She described a plump, balding, older man, possibly some kind of mentor. There was a teenage girl, her throat slit. Another female entity entered the room; she was a cold and dark presence. Her head hanging down, she crouched in a corner. The same person murdered all these people. They are trying to tell you that you are on the right track and that you must be careful. If you claim to them that you want to know, they will follow you around to make you see the truth. With the victims so willing to come through, Mariah was convinced that the séance would be successful.

Mariah used the Tarot cards to tap into the spirit world. After pulling the first card, the Page of Wands, she warned Katherine that she was in danger. It was at this point that Katherine showed her book. "Does this book rest at the bottom of our problems?" she pulled a card. The answer was "yes." "What do we most need to know?" she asked the cards.

Mariah described a ghost that was engulfed with guilt, one who was trying to keep Katherine from harm. Mariah explained that when someone commits suicide it is the most unforgivable sin except when one who kills themselves and takes the lives of others, they are the damned! Here, attached to the ring, was a ghost that feels responsible for the deaths caused by this killer. "Does this ring belong to this person" the cards replied, "yes." Mariah also, detected a spirit trying to stop this spirit, one who was trying to confuse Katherine efforts. Katherine pulled another card, asking for a message. The card she pulled indicated that the message would come through very soon. "Am I in physical danger?" She pulled another card. The five of pentacles indicated a physical loss but not necessarily death. Mariah believed that there was a killer that was still alive. She also believed that he could be stalking her. Mariah told us that the ghost attached to the ring was trying to redeem himself through helping Katherine.

Mariah warned us that we had not prepared properly to conduct the séance. Spiritual preparation for a séance includes a complete fast for three days and a partial fast for nine days. We needed two mediums, one the "doorway" and one the "battery." She also warned of spirits who might appear to our left. These would be abominations, those that haunt!

She said it was too late for us to do the traditional salt cleansing which starts on the dark of the moon. "There should be a seven-day ritual, covering the body with sea salt, including the hair and bottoms of the feet. Then shower after an hour." "You must also say a cleansing prayer," she informed us, and any one that is familiar would do. We would need seven to nine people for a séance. She also told us that the best time for a séance is the first through full moon phase. Even though we were a little off on some of the normal requirements, it felt right. We had recently celebrated St. John's Eve and the Summer Solstice, so I knew that the veil was still rather thin -- a good time for communication with the dead.

We chose Southern Nights, a spiritually active property, as the location of our séance. The locations of the ley lines were appropriate, as well. We carefully chose who would be involved. We had Mariah and her husband, who served as the two mediums, Katherine, and myself. Added to that were two very experienced psychics, Seth and Mimi, who were highly sensitive channels. Tour company owner Sidney Smith made number seven.

We met with Mariah early in the day to get herbs for a cleansing bath. She carefully chose those that would open us up for channeling. "Not too much, though," she warned. Too much could have an effect similar to alcohol. It could also make us too vulnerable to the spirits. There must be a balance when it comes to doing such delicate work. If one opens up too much to spirits, it could be dangerous. There are elemental spirits who are constantly earthbound seeking human hosts to invade. "Have one of them get inside of you, then you have trouble," Mariah warned. "It's a lot less work avoiding such things rather than attempting to rid oneself of it."

Upon entering the gate at Southern Nights, we each noticed that someone had placed a small stuffed doll at the entrance. This seemed to be no accident. When Seth and Mimi had arrived, they explained that this was a very old Voodoo custom. Somehow, someone knew what we were going to be doing that evening. Whoever that someone was, they were attempting to protect us!

We began to prepare the room for the séance. While several of us removed the table setting, Mariah anointed the appropriate candles. The oils that Mimi used to enhance the connection were so strong that she had to wear rubber gloves, taking care not to make contact with her skin. Once everything was set up, we gathered around and held hands. Mariah warned us not to break the connection, as it would create an opening for the spirits to enter one of us.

After only a few short minutes, Mariah became aware of several entities that had joined us. She recognized some from earlier that day in my office. The room grew colder as the spirits entered and surrounded us. The older, bald man had returned, and took his place at Katherine's side. Others crowded around. A dark ominous spirit stood behind Seth. We believed this had been the one Katherine was searching for. We all sensed that this was our vampire! However, he never revealed this to us directly.

Cecelia, the resident ghost of Southern Nights, was standing in the corner of the room. It was as if she were watching over us to make sure all went well. We asked several questions of the spirits but there seemed to be some resistance at first. We waited patiently.

Within time, we began to channel the spirits. I became engulfed with an icy embrace, my arms tingling. The dark female spirit had wrapped around me. I could feel her icy chill absorbing my entire being! My bones literally ached from the cold. As I told the others what I was experiencing, I could feel my throat tightening. My voice was weakening and becoming faint as I struggled to utter the tiniest of sounds. I felt like I was being strangled! Knowing she had died feeling intense fear, I suddenly had a flash in my mind's eye as to what had befallen her. Two men had beaten her. Then, just before slashing her throat, she watched them destroy her pet dog! She had screamed and screamed until she could no more. Then they killed her.

At that point, Mimi began to channel another spirit. This one was male. She felt as if her throat was being torn open. Intense pain gripped her as tears welled up in her eyes. She commanded the spirit to leave her; it was too much to bear. It was at this time that the dark one began to channel through Seth. Laughing at us, and at the other entities, he became louder. Seth's body shuddered. His face was almost frozen with terror as the entity spoke through him. As he boasted loudly, the coldness of the female entity abruptly left me and was replaced by a feeling of safety. "Michael is here," I announced.

Katherine looked up with astonishment. It was the one we called the mentor. He was the Vampire instructor. He ordered the dark one to be quiet and leave.

We all realized at this point that the ring had probably been his. Our vampire killer most likely took it from him when murdering him, then proceeded to wear it himself. She recalled that a psychic in another state had mentioned his name when touching the ring. She hadn't realized that he was the entity that had been with her all along, protecting her. The dark one sulked away silently and then the others left as well. We had accomplished a lot in one sitting and felt drained of energy. We closed the circle.

The following day, I was completely exhausted. The intense day of investigations followed by the séance was beginning to take a toll on my energy level. The exhaustion and negative feelings stayed with me for about two weeks after the incident. It was during this period in time that I worked with the EVP. The voice that I had recorded was that of one of the victims. Although Mariah offered to attempt to get rid of the entity, I chose to allow him to stay as long as he wished; to work things out for himself.

Seth suffered several mara attacks for about a week after the gathering. He was experiencing the attacks around 5:00 a.m. The only thing that helped him was to keep busy all night and to sleep during the day. Eventually, the attacks ceased. Mimi had gotten sporadic messages from the dark entity through her readings and in her dreams. Several days after the séance, she even had an experience with the entity sending her cryptic messages on her computer screen. I believe that we opened a channel by wanting to know the truth. These spirits are now going to make sure we hear them and that we do not give up or forget they exist. They want their justice.

I spoke with Mariah a couple of days later. She claimed to have had choking feelings since the séance, declaring that the one with the slit throat had been following her. She talked with another spiritualist and noted that she never saw the dark one's face. Mariah's feeling is that he may never have been human at all, perhaps being a wandering demon. I mentioned that his alleged human accomplice has had another spirit companion. She heard a voice the next day proclaim, "You think it has stopped but it hasn't."

Mariah was determined, however, that she was not going to allow it to bother her. He did not belong with her and she refused to further acknowledge his presence. Katherine went back home the day after the séance. Most of the entities departed with her as well. After all, they were her ghosts to begin with. She continued to work with them, attempting to communicate. To my knowledge, her vampire ghost still haunts her.

Closing

On August 29, 2005, New Orleans became the target of the largest natural disaster known to America, Hurricane Katrina. Since then, many businesses in the area have closed down and many residents have moved away. While visitors to the area have shown a great deal of compassion for those who suffered losses in the storm, they have also expressed a curiosity as to the storm's effect on paranormal activity in New Orleans.

Many lives were taken by Katrina throughout New Orleans and the Gulf Coast region. To our knowledge, there were no deaths in the areas where our tours take place. Still, the tragedy seems to have affected those spirits who reside here as well. Directly after Katrina, there was a strange void that seemed to envelope the entire city. From an energetic standpoint, I can only describe feeling as emptiness. Normally, New Orleans has a particular pulse to it. After Katrina, that pulse was missing.

In those early days, I had to wonder if New Orleans was ever going to be what it was. I contacted a psychic I work with for some insight. She told me that she had been visited by a spirit that appeared only as a shadow. The shadow told her only that the dead in New Orleans were accustomed to being given a lot of attention and energy, and right now, they were as lost and hungry as the living. This made me realize that those spirits did experience the loss of something when the city shut down. Perhaps, like myself, they wondered if it would return to normal.

Fortunately, we have been able to experience New Orleans coming back to life. We have no way of knowing how long it will take to rebuild what once was. But the pulse is back, beating stronger than ever. The spirit of New Orleans continues to live and breathe, and as always attract those curious of its wonders. We are grateful for its survival and honor those who crossed over untimely due to this tragedy.

Tour guide Bill Arendell surrounded by tour
participants during a Haunted History Tour

Epilogue

$\mathcal{M}$any of the stories that you have just read are from our French Quarter Ghosts and Legends, Ghosts of the Garden District, Voodoo, and Vampire Tours. They have been researched extensively and are backed by actual documentation, and whenever possible, photographic evidence. Personal accounts given to us have not been altered.

Although some may sound bizarre, they are nonetheless what have been relayed to us by the people who have experienced them. In some cases, we have refrained from using names or have changed names to protect those who preferred not to be identified. We remain committed to providing the most accurate information and documentation on our tours. Constant research and factual updates guarantee these stories will never be stale. Our presentations are theatrical, informative, and fun. Many people leave the city feeling that our tours were the highlight of their trip. Often, visitors will take these tours year after year to hear the updated information.

So, if you should ever find yourself in New Orleans and happen to see something whisk by in the corner of your eye; or you brush past a cold figure that isn't there, or perhaps some dark, mysterious stranger with piercing eyes asks for a light... take a deep breath and remind yourself that such things do exist, especially in New Orleans.

For information on my other books or videos, please visit my web site at www.kalilasmith.com

PARAPSYCHOLOGY TERMS

Altered State of Consciousness (ASC)
A term used to refer to any state of consciousness that is different from "normal" states of waking or sleeping. ASCs include hypnosis, trance, ecstasy, psychedelic and meditative experience. ASCs do not necessarily have paranormal features.

Apparition
The visual appearance of an entity whose physical body is not present. Generally, an apparition applies to any form of entity where it is distinguishable as a person or animal. The apparition can appear in partial or full-bodied.

Apport / Asport
An apport is a solid object that seemingly appears from nowhere in the presence of a medium. Asport is any object the "spirits" or medium makes disappear or teleports to another location.

Astral body
The body a person seems to occupy during an out-of-body experience.

Astral Plane
A world some people believe exists above the physical world.

Astral projection
An out-of-body experience.

Astrology
A theory and practice which attempts to identify the ways in which astronomical events are correlated with events on earth.

Aura
A field that some psychics see surrounding the living body.

Automatic Writing
Writing without being aware of the contents, as when a medium apparently transcribes written messages from disembodied spirits.

Automatism

Any unconscious and spontaneous muscular movement caused by "the spirits."(Automatic writing).

Bilocation

Being (or appearing to be) in two different places at the same time.

Card Guessing

Experimental tests for ESP in which subjects guess the identity of a set of cards.

Cerebral Anoxia

Lack of oxygen to the brain, often causing sensory distortions and hallucinations. Sometimes used to explain features of the near-death experience.

Chakra

An energy center in the human body, which processes psychic energies and abilities.

Channeling

The process by which a medium apparently allows a spirit to communicate through his or her person.

Clairaudience

Auditory form of ESP (compare with Clairvoyance).

Clairsentience

Physical sensations (or smell) form of ESP. Sometimes used as a general term for clairvoyance and clairaudience.

Clairvoyance

A subset of ESP. The viewing of distant scenes not apparent to the eye, may appear externally - either replacing the normal visual scene (visions) or being incorporated into it (as could be the case with apparitions) - or internally, in the form of mental imagery and intuition.

Closed Deck

A set of cards used in a card-guessing test where each card appears a fixed number of times. Statistical analysis of research data using a closed deck differs from statistical analysis of data using an open deck.

Cold Reading
A technique using a series of general statements, questions, and answers that allows fake mediums, mind-readers, and magicians to obtain previously unknown information about a person. (In a Cold Reading, the reader has no prior knowledge).

Collective Apparition
An unusual type of "ghost" sighting in which more than one person sees the same phenomenon.

Control
In experimental parapsychology a procedure undertaken in order to ensure that the experiment is conducted in a standard fashion and so that results are not unduly influenced by extraneous factors.

Crisis Apparition
An apparition is seen when the subject is at the point of death or is the victim of a serious illness or injury.

Curse
To speak a wish of evil against someone or call down forces to hurt someone.

Demon
An evil spirit that was never human.

Discarnate
Spirits that exist without a physical body.

Ectoplasm
A substance which emanates from the body of a medium during a trance. This often appears as a mist-like substance.

Electromagnetic Field
A field propagated by a combination of electric and magnetic energy, which radiates from radio and light waves to gamma and cosmic rays. It is believed that when spirits manifest, they create an electromagnetic field.

EMF Detector
An instrument that measures electromagnetic energy. Also known as a Gauss Meter or magnetometer.

ESP
ESP or extrasensory perception is considered what scientists refer to as a receptive psi. This type of experience usually involves the transfer of information.

EVP
Electronic voice phenomena. Voices captured on audiotape when no one is present. It is believed that these voices are from spirits attempting to communicate with living people.

Experiment
A test carried out under controlled conditions.

Experimental Group
A group of subjects who undergo a specific experimental procedure. Often results from this group are compared with those of a control group.

Experimental Parapsychology
Parapsychology research involving experimental methods rather than survey techniques or the investigation of spontaneous cases.

Experimenter
The person who conducts the experiment.

Experimenter Effect
Influence that the experimenter's personality or behavior may have on the results of an experiment.

False Awakening
An experience in which a person believes he or she has woken up, but actually is still dreaming.

Forced Choice Experiment
An experiment in which the subject is forced to choose among an assortment of possible targets, such as the five ESP cards.

Free Response Experiment
An experiment in which the subject knows only the general nature of the target.

Ganzfield Experiment
An experiment where input from the outside world is reduced by placing halved ping-pong balls over the eyes and by masking external sounds. A state of mild sensory deprivation.

Ghost
A form of apparition, usually the visual appearance of a deceased human's 'spirit soul' or that of a crisis apparition.

Ghost Hunt / Ghost Investigation
A ghost hunt is an informal attempt to simply sight or record a "ghost" in a location similar to others known to be haunted. A ghost investigation, on the other hand, is a carefully controlled research project, set up to record paranormal activity, usually at a location known, or presumed to be haunted.

Goat
A subject in an experiment who does not believe in the ability for which he or she is being tested.

Hallucination
Perception of sights, sounds, etc., that are not actually present. Ghosts, as we define them, are not hallucinations, because they have a real, external cause.

Haunting
Recurrent sounds of human activity, sightings of apparitions, and other psychic phenomena, in a location when no one is there physically.

Hypnosis
Sleeplike state in which the subject acts only on external suggestion.

Illusion
A distorted perception of objects or events causing a discrepancy between what is perceived and what is reality.

Incline Effect
An increase in performance on a psi test when the test is repeated.

Intuition
The non-paranormal ability to grasp the elements of a situation or to draw conclusions about complex events in ways that go beyond a purely rational or intellectual analysis.

Judge
Person who compares targets and responses in a psi experiment.

Kirlian Photography
A photographic method involving high frequency electric current, discovered by S.D. & V. Kirlian in the Soviet Union. Kirlian photographs often show colored halos or "auras" surrounding objects.

Laying on of Hands
A process by which certain healers profess to be able to heal patients by touch.

Levitation
The lifting of physical objects by psychokinesis (PK).

Life Review
Flashback memories of the whole of a person's life often associated with the near-death experience.

Longbody
A web of living connections among people, places, and objects.

Lucid Dreaming
Dreaming in which the person is aware that the experience is a dream. Often associated with feelings of aliveness and freedom, and with the ability to control dream events.

Materialization
The deliberate, usually temporary, visible and/or physical formation of a spirit.

Medium
A psychic through who spirits can communicate. There are two types of mediums: light and deep trance.

Medium (direct voice)
A trance medium that apparently acts as a transmitter for the voices of disembodied spirits.

Medium (materialization)
A medium that seems to be able to give physical form to the deceased from a substance called "ectoplasm."

Metaphysics
Derived from the Latin word "meta" which means "beyond," metaphysics would literally mean that which is beyond the laws of physics. The study of psychical research.

NDE
Near death experience. Experienced when the person is in fact clinically dead for a period of time. The person usually feels himself or herself leaving their body and sometimes observing the location and people around them, they usually often view their own lifeless bodies, then the person feels as though they are rising up through some sort of tunnel towards a bright light. Sometimes they may see or hear a deceased family member or friend, or even a religious figure of some kind. The person having this experience is usually told it is not the right time, or they decide themselves it is not time to die, and they return to their bodies.

OBE
Out of body experience, or astral projection. This is the sensation or experience many people have of actually leaving their body for a period of time, this is where the spirit or soul leaves the body. This can also be described as "traveling clairvoyance."

Orb
A sphere of electromagnetic energy produced by spirits. Also called a globule.

Ouija Board
Game board manufactured by the Parker Brothers Company. Used to

communicate with spirits. Some believe this "communication" is caused by the collective unconscious of the participants.

Paranormal
Occurrences that take place outside the natural order of things. This would include ghosts, UFO's, ESP and other things difficult to explain by nature but in the realm of the natural.

Parapsychology
The branch of science that studies psychic phenomena.

Percipient
A person who sees an apparition or ghost.

Phenomenology
An approach to research that aims to describe and clarify a person's own experience and understanding of an event or phenomenon.

Poltergeist
A German word meaning "noisy or rowdy ghost."

PK - Psychokinesis
The power of the mind to affect matter without physical contact.

Place memory
Information about past events that apparently is stored in the physical environment.

Precognition
The ability to predict things beyond present knowledge.

Psi
A letter in the Greek alphabet that denotes psychic phenomena.

Psyche
The Greek word for "self," "mind," or "soul."

Psychic
A person with above average ESP abilities.

Psychic Healing
A mode of healing affected by the psychic abilities of the healer.

Psychic Surgery
The supposed ability to paranormally perform invasive surgery using no conventional medical tools.

Psychometry
ESP of events associated with inanimate objects.

Quantitative Method
A research method involving the collection and statistical analysis of numerical data.

Qualitative Method
A research method involving the collection of non-quantitative data (e.g., observations, interviews, subjective reports, case studies).

Quantitative Method
A research method involving the collection and statistical analysis of numerical data.

Remote Viewing
(1)Another term for clairvoyance.(2)An ESP procedure in which a percipient attempts to become aware psychically of the experience of an agent who is at a distant, unknown target location.

REM
Rapid eye movement during sleep that indicates dreaming.

Repressed Psychokinetic Energy
A theoretical psychic force produced, usually unconsciously, by an individual undergoing physical or mental trauma. When released, the power causes paranormal occurrences such as poltergeist activity.

Retrocognition
The awareness of objects and events that existed in a past time

RSPK
Recurrent spontaneous psychokinesis. A possible cause of apparent

poltergeist activity.

Sceptic (skeptic)
A person inclined to discount the reality of the paranormal and to be critical of parapsychological research. Generally seeks rational or scientific explanations for the phenomenon studied by parapsychologists.

Scrying
A term used to cover a wide range of divination techniques which parapsychology would tend to classify as types of ESP. Most scrying techniques involve some degree of fixation on a surface with a clear optical depth or on an area, which shows random patterns, the idea being that subconscious information available to the scrying will be manifested in their interpretation of the imagery or random patterns they see.

Séance
A group of people who gather in an effort to communicate with the dead.

Sensitive
A person with psychic abilities.

Shadow Ghost
A black, mist like spirit that has no discernable features. It is usually demonic in nature and is sometimes described by witnesses as a "black shape".

Shaman
A 'wizard' in tribal societies who is an intermediary between the living, the dead, and the gods.

Sheep
A subject in an experiment who believes in the ability for which he or she is being tested.

Spirit Photography
A spirit photograph captures the image of a ghost on film. Many of these are supposedly intended as a mere portrait of a living human being, but when the film is developed, an ethereal ghostly face or figure can be seen hovering near the subject. This may also incorporate orbs, vortexes, and mists to some degree.

Spirit Theater
A term used by modern-day magicians to describe shows, acts, or tricks in which ghosts or other spirit activity are apparently produced.

Spiritualism
A belief system that "spirits" of the dead can (and do) communicate with living humans in the material world.

Subjective Apparitions
Apparitions or phenomena that are hallucinations created by our minds.

Stigmata
Unexplained markings on a person's body that correspond to the wounds of Christ.

Supernatural
Something that exists or occurs through some means other than any known force in nature. As opposed to paranormal, the term "supernatural" often connotes divine or demonic intervention.

Telekinesis
Paranormal movement of objects.

Telepathy
The direct passing of information from one mind to another.

Teleportation
A kind of paranormal transportation in which an object is moved from one distinct location to another, often through a solid object such as a wall.

Temporal Lobe Activity
Electrical activity in the temporal lobes of the brain. Often associated with strange sensations, time distortions and hallucinations. Sometimes used as an explanation for seemingly paranormal experiences such as apparitions.

Thought Form
An apparition produced by the power of the human mind.

Trance
A sleeplike state in which there is a change of consciousness.

Vortex (vortice)
A photographed anomaly that appears as a funnel o that is not seen at the time of the photograph that supposedly represents a "ghost."

White Noise
A hiss-like sound, formed by compiling all audible frequencies.

Selected Bibliography and Resources

Beautiful Crescent A History of New Orleans, Joan B. Garvey and Mary Widmer; Garmer Press 1994

New Orleans Ghosts, Victor C. Klein; Lycanthrope Press 1996

Haunted Louisiana, Christy L. Viviano; Tree House Press 1992

The Afterlife, Jenny Randles and Peter Hough; Berkley Books, 1994

Haunted Bayou and other Cajun Ghost Stories, J.J. Reneaux; August House Publishers, 1994

The Unquiet Dead, Dr. Edith Fiore; Ballantine Books

Life After Life, Raymond A. Moody; Mockingbird Press

Ghost Stories of Old New Orleans, Jeanne de Lavigne; Rinehart & Company, Inc. 1946

Beyond Death's Door, Maurice Rawlings, M.D.; Bantam Books, 1971

Paranormal Experience and the Survival of Death, Carl B. Becker; State University of New York Press, 1993

The Vampire Book, The Encyclopedia of the Undead, J. Gordon Melton;

Liquid Dreams of Vampires, Martin v. Riccardo; Llewellyn Publications, 1996

The Killers Among Us, Colin Wilson and Damon Wilson; Warner Books, 1995

Vampires: The Occult Truth, Konstantinos; Llewellyn Publications, 1996

Times-Picayune Article, October 3, 1863, February 2, 1864, May 1, 1864,

December 11, 1868, June 26, 1874, June 22, 1890, August 20, 1890,

November 13, 1950, October 7, 1951, March 7, 1952

The Complete Vampire Companion, Rosemary Ellen Guilley; MacMillan, 1994

Vampires, Burial, and Death, Paul Barber; Yale University Press, 1988

Times- Picayune, February 11, 1979, "Sultan's House: Life with an Exotic Ghost," Lorena Durea

Times-Picayune, October 25, 1989, "Historic Haunts: A Halloween Visit with Ghosts in the Quarter," Millie Ball

Piercing the Darkness, Undercover with Vampires in America Today, Katherine Ramsland, Harper Prism, 1998

The Voodoo Queen, Robert Tallant, Pelican Publishing, 1984

Voodoo & Hoodoo, Jim Haskins; Scarborough House, 1978

Voodoo; Past & Present, Ron Bodin; University of Southwestern Louisiana, 1990

Carnival of the Spirit, Luisha Teish; Harper San Francisco, 1994

A Brief History of Voodoo: Slavery & Survival of the African Gods; A.P. Antippas, Hembco, 1988

Divine Horsemen: The Living Gods of Haiti; Maya Deren, McPherson & Company, 1953

Voodoo In New Orleans, Robert Tallant; Pelican Publishing, 1983

Acknowledgments:

I would like to thank all of the residents, business owners, and staff who cooperated with our investigations to make this book possible. I also extend my gratitude to those who shared their personal accounts and photographs with us. In addition, I want to express my warm appreciation to Mariah and her husband, Fuzzy, and particularly, Katherine Ramsland for stepping out into the "other side" with me. I believe our journey will continue with the doors that we have opened. I would like to recognize all of our assistants and tour guides on the Haunted History Research Team for their contributions.

And last but certainly not least, a very special thank you to all who submitted photographs to be included in this book. The book would not have been the same without them.